MW00324849

Also by Carol Geiler

Books

Surviving Spiritual Emergence: A Personal Story of Spiritual & Psychic Awakening With Tips on How to Survive These Life-Changing Events

(Coming Winter 2016)

Website & Blog

www.carolgeiler.com

www.spiritualpotentialnow.com

SPIRIT ACTIVITY

WHAT IS IT

&

WHAT TO DO ABOUT IT

By

CAROL GEILER

LEGAL NOTES

THIS BOOK IS NOT INTENDED AS A SUBSTITUTE FOR THE MEDICAL ADVICE OF PHYSICIANS. THE READER SHOULD REGULARLY CONSULT A PHYSICIAN IN MATTERS RELATING TO HIS/HER HEALTH AND PARTICULARLY WITH RESPECT TO ANY SYMPTOMS THAT MAY REQUIRE DIAGNOSIS OR MEDICAL ATTENTION. THE AUTHOR DOES NOT DISPENSE MEDICAL ADVICE OR PRESCRIBE THE USE OF ANY TECHNIQUES AS A FORM OF TREATMENT FOR PHYSICAL, EMOTIONAL, OR MEDICAL PROBLEMS WITHOUT THE ADVICE OF A MEDICAL PROFESSIONAL. THE INTENT OF THE AUTHOR IS TO OFFER INFORMATION OF A GENERAL NATURE TO HELP YOU IN YOUR QUEST FOR FINDING ANSWERS REGARDING YOUR SPIRITUAL EXPERIENCES AND GROWTH.

TABLE OF CONTENTS

INTRODUCTION
SPIRIT ACTIVITY

There are things that go bump in the night, items that seem to fly off the walls or break on their own, disembodied voices, chills, cold spots, visual distortions, strange lights, shadows, creaking floors, and more. There are also times when a presence is felt or sensed or voices are heard internally, but not in the physical environment. Then there are those very rare instances when events may become more personal, and people claim to be attacked, scratched, haunted, held down, or even possessed.

Often referred to as "paranormal," these unexplained events are quickly labeled as "spirit activity" by many people who experience them. But what spirit activity is real and what is the result of belief, imagination, or even physiological or psychological causes? Differentiating among these can be very tough, and there are a variety of reasons for this confusion.

American television has made spirit activity a thing of curiosity, sparking people's interest in the topic, but also offering sensationalism instead of education. In addition, religion and personal ideologies can also limit our understanding of these events, sometimes making them seem impossible, negative, or even socially unacceptable. We may snicker and sneer when someone says they "saw a ghost," but what happens to those people who truly believe they're having such encounters? Real or imagined, there's little valuable assistance available, and a lack of education and openness only perpetuates fear, misunderstanding, ridicule, and judgment.

What are we to do?

People often turn to psychics, paranormal groups, or religious representatives. After all, if we believe we're having spirit activity or contact, then why wouldn't we seek out someone who can support our issues rather than judge and condemn them? Unfortunately, these sources aren't always as helpful or as supportive as we'd like them to be.

When it comes to religious representatives, even those who preach and speak about God and a spiritual life may officially ignore and discount the existence of spirits. If they do believe in spirits, they may still discount the spirits' ability to affect or interact with the living. The notion is dismissed as purely fantastical or as a psychological issue they aren't willing or able to deal with — or worse yet, is only seen as evil.

Paranormal groups can be little better. Some are thrill-seeking, hoping to see or experience something for their own self-gratification rather than being focused on the educational and assistive aspect of the work. Groups also widely vary on their theories and ideologies and mainly exist as hobbyist centers for those who share a common passion for the paranormal.

Psychics also have a wide range of beliefs, experiences, and explanations, not all of which are founded in truth or reality. There are the easy-to-find dime-store psychics who will peddle fluff and then there are the more serious, genuine, and talented ones who tend to be quieter. Fear of ridicule, doubt, skepticism and other considerations keeps them doing their work diligently, but not always loudly.

Our personalities have a lot to do with how we handle these potential spirit-related events. Some are fearful, others excited and happy, while a few may become protective and will boldly take control of their personal space and environment without needing or wanting assistance. Then there are those who remain in complete denial or disbelief until things get so bad they're forced to deal with them. We are free to choose how to deal with the claimed activity, but no matter our approach, the wide range of emotional concerns typically need to be dealt with in order to successfully move forward in life — whether the activity is valid or not.

Because of all of these factors, gaining assistance for the emergence of spirit activity can be a very frightening, as well as frustrating, process. As a result, this Resource Guide was designed to assist people in the discernment and education process. It offers various possibilities for why spirit activity may be occurring and also includes a variety of educational resources to help people start their own journey towards finding answers. Unfortunately, there's no quick-fix, and many people will have to deal with the activity for a period of time before a final resolution is found. By learning key steps to help you examine the problem as well as resolve it, you can feel better equipped to handle the events in a calm, rational, and successful manner.

As you read the information provided, try to choose the scenarios that seem to fit your own personal situation, noting one or more may apply. Remember to stay open and consider all possible options. If you feel you're too scared or too unsure to work alone and you want to contact someone who can help you, this Guide also provides valuable tips for seeking outside assistance.

Additionally, if you're someone who enjoys assisting others with these matters, then this Guide can help you develop an objective process for doing so. You may want to suggest your clients also acquire the Guide so you can work through it together, or you can use it as a tool to help you develop a process that fits into your own unique line of work.

As someone who has worked closely with spirit communication since 2008 and been a member of the Washington State Ghost Society since 2012, I not only understand from personal experience how troubling perceived spirit activity can be, but I've also encountered a barrage of emails from other people who are plagued with the same questions and events. As an Intuitive and Medium I come from a believer's perspective. My life has shown me that there's more to the world than meets the eye, and I can't turn from that. Despite this, I also work to diligently guard against making sweeping claims regarding true spirit activity. I value my professional reputation and seek to balance belief with skeptical objectivity.

The line between spiritual and physical reality is a thin one, and there is a world of people curious to understand more about their experiences but lacking knowledge of how to proceed.

I hope you'll find this Resource Guide useful in your journey.

Carol L Geiler

CHAPTER 1
LOOKING FOR ANSWERS

Determining if spirit activity is real can be a very tough and delicate matter. Our experiences and beliefs are extremely powerful. Once convinced of a given conclusion we tend to hang on to that decision until the bitter end, even when it's false and flies in the face of scientific fact. For example, maybe we've just watched a TV show about the paranormal and suddenly a picture frame slips from the wall and falls to the floor. We make a conclusion, based on the timing of this event, that perhaps it's Aunt Martha since it's her picture. This isn't to say it's **not** Aunt Martha, but oftentimes objectivity goes out the window when we're convinced something is going on, or when we **want** it to be going on. Desire for connection and interaction can appear to give rise to spirit activity; however, this still doesn't mean its occurrence is legitimate.

There are often many rational explanations for certain events which are attributed to spirits. Some events are caused by environmental factors while others may have physiological and/or psychological roots. Even when our experiences are truly caused by actual spirit activity, we need to be sure we're considering **all** possibilities. Remaining objective is tough, but it's critically essential when dealing with these matters. When and if you find yourself in a situation so overwhelming and intrusive that objectivity simply isn't possible, then it may be time to look for support. There are two avenues you should consider: **medical support** and **spiritual support**.

Medical Support

I can't stress enough how important medical assistance can be during this process, especially if you're feeling emotionally, mentally, and/or physically overwhelmed or unbalanced. If you're being consumed to the point you're unable to function, then seek professional help. I encourage you to utilize people who can help so that you can regain control of your life. Many so-called spirit-related events can be very rationally explained by medical conditions, so allow yourself to pursue this avenue before coming to any final conclusions about what's really going on.

If you would like to find psychological assistance, then you may want to consider looking for people in the Transpersonal Psychology field. This branch of psychology works with individuals who are experiencing issues with spiritual emergence, an awakening of the self to something beyond the physical. Not all of these emergence issues deal with actual spirit activity or contact, but the therapeutic process may help you discern what type of activity is occurring. Transpersonal psychologists invaluably allow for the impact of the spiritual experience to have relevance, and indeed, this is one of the focal aspects of their therapies.

Another psychological resource is the Spiritual Emergence Network. These are also therapists who are open to those undergoing spiritual-related events. However, notice I said *spiritual* and not *spirit*. Belief in the two may or may not go hand in hand, but at least you can speak to someone who will be open to your experiences and should serve as an unbiased professional resource. They will not validate your experiences or encourage them, simply help you asses and evaluate.

When seeking physiological assistance, start with your Primary Care doctor and find out if he/she would suggest you see a specialist. Their recommendations will depend on the types of symptoms/activity you're dealing with. These might be sleep-related, neurological, or caused by other minor illnesses. Be honest with your doctor about what's going on and allow them to thoroughly help you determine some potential physiological causes. If nothing else, you'll eliminate what's *not* the cause, which can help put your mind at ease and reinforce the validity of any genuine spirit-related issues.

If these options are just too darn scary or you don't have the resources to seek out a medical professional, then take some time to research your events and symptoms. Don't leap to study only the spiritual causes without also considering physical ones. The internet is full of information, so do a little digging and see if what you're experiencing has any foundations in psychological or physiological causes.

Spiritual Support

In addition to support from the medical community, you may also want to look for someone whom I refer to as a *Spiritual Advocate*. Since the medical community is not always very open to the possibility of spirit activity, you may want to seek out a person or persons who can assist you with the spiritual side of things. Whether the activity is valid or not, someone who believes in its existence will be better able to help you grapple with the questions and emotions your experience has provoked. They can offer a perspective which may be comforting and will allow the potential for the experience to be real.

A word of caution: just as the medical community may be closed-minded about spirit activity, some Spiritual Advocates may fall on the opposite end of the spectrum and believe too readily. They may be all too willing to jump to the conclusion that the activity is real, as their own beliefs and concepts are often as firmly held as those of their medical counterparts. Make sure that your Advocate understands the value of seeking medical assistance in conjunction with the spiritual and is the type of person who can remain not only supportive, but more importantly, objective.

So who can we use as a Spiritual Advocate?

Some people turn to paranormal groups. After all, they're supposed to be the experts on ghosts and spirits, right? But every group is unique, having their own ideologies and theories. Some are out to have personal encounters and tend to utilize those in need of assistance as a way to gain them. They're seeking their own proof in the form of physical manifestations (which may or may not occur with every spirit-related issue), and they may be using a client's experiences to obtain these opportunities. Some groups may be very willing to investigate, but leave offering little education, resolution, or follow-up. Obviously, this is far from helpful.

There are also some paranormal groups who utilize Mediums and Psychics, sometimes called Sensitives or Intuitives. These groups have an opposing viewpoint to the aforementioned groups, tending to believe in spirit activity without requiring physical evidence. But, they may make assumptions that everything is spirit-related without being objective and considering some of the more practical explainable causes.

If you opt for a paranormal group to assist you, then be sure to read their website. This will give you a clue if they're skeptics or believers. One type of group is not better than the other, they simply differ in their views, and thus, their approach. If you do choose a group, then you should interview them carefully so you'll know what to expect. A well-organized and established organization should have a process and be able to explain this to their clients quickly and easily. To help you with this I've provided a list of potential interview questions in the Appendix.

So how do you find a group? The best way is to search online for paranormal groups or societies. The internet lists many groups who provide services, but some may be inactive. Paranormal groups and societies come and go over time, so you'll want to email to find out if the group is still current.

When making a final selection you may have to wade through a sea of groups until you find the one that resonates with you, but then again you may find there aren't any in your area. It all just depends on where you live. If you can't find a local group, then you can try contacting some more distant ones. They may be willing to work with you through email or phone. Granted, this is not as ideal as having them come to your home, but it still may offer you an opportunity to get some assistance.

The last thing I'll mention about paranormal groups is that they're made up of volunteers and function more like clubs than anything else. There's no legal entity governing the groups, and the paranormal as a cultural phenomenon has attracted many people who are simply curious. That's not to say there aren't avid and passionate truth-seekers out there, because there are, and some of them have been doing this work long before TV shows made it an attraction. Just realize that groups vary in their intent. In addition, those who are serious also tend to be limited in their resources and so simply don't have the ability to serve everyone who contacts them. Don't get discouraged if a group makes you go through an interview process or can't assist you immediately or even in the future. Keep searching for answers and other groups who may be able to offer you some insights.

Another type of Spiritual Advocate is a Medium, Psychic, Sensitive, or Intuitive. All of these words are often used interchangeably although there are subtle differences in their meanings. These are people who can supposedly communicate with and/or perceive what is imperceptible to most. This sensitivity may include sensing or communicating with spirits or simply picking up on general energy, emotions, feelings, thoughts, and images. But as with the paranormal groups, we must ask if they can be objective while also supportive and educational in their approach.

You can search online for these Intuitive types of Advocates using any of the above-mentioned titles, but how do you know who to trust? One of the best ways is through word of mouth, but if you're afraid to ask around then you'll be forced to use the internet. Make sure a potential contact's website is professional and kept up-to-date. Email them to see if they provide a prompt, polite, professional, and well-written response. A 24-hour turnaround time or less is typically what you're looking for. Check their site for testimonials and additional information about how they work. Once you've narrowed down your choices you may want to ask to speak to them in person. I've provided a list of some potential interview questions in the Appendix.

A third type of Spiritual Advocate you may want to use is someone who shares your religious views. This may be a priest, pastor, rabbi, imam, guru, monk, nun, yogi, shaman, and so on. While most Intuitive types consider themselves more spiritual than religious, finding someone who shares your personal religious views may put you at greater ease. Of course, every religion has its own ideas regarding spirit contact and/or activity. And while I can't say how they'll all respond, I know from my own very staunch Christian upbringing that the presence of spirits is typically viewed in some faith traditions as either evil or impossible. If, however, this type of Advocate feels right to you, then they may serve as an excellent resource. Just remember, not all practitioners are the same, so you may need to look around until you find that religious Advocate who can be open and helpful while still remaining within your preferred religious framework.

A Spiritual Advocate can also simply be a friend or loved one. Granted this may be hard for them, since most people have very decided beliefs about spirits. Will they believe you, belittle you, or just humor you? Even if they truly want to help, they may not know how. Still, it's good to have trusted friends to talk to. Sharing and speaking freely about what's going on is a great source of comfort and release of emotional tension and stress, so if you have someone who can fit this role, then be sure to talk with them about these matters. Just remember, however, that while they may be supportive and helpful, they may lack some of the resources and know-how to help you gain resolution.

Now that you have an insight into how to gain support and assistance from the medical and spiritual communities, you might be wondering what you can do in the meantime. Is it really necessary to go to the extreme of seeking medical or spiritual help right away? After all, you're looking for answers on a topic that people don't want to talk about or will scoff at if you do. The experience can be scary for deeply personal reasons, so what can you do?

The decisions can be overwhelming! I know from experience, not only in my own life, but also through serving as an Investigator and Medium for the Washington State Ghost Society. Time and time again I've come across frantic people who want and need help but don't know what to do and aren't ready to take the leap to seek outside help. That's why I created this Resource Guide: to offer some basic tools and concepts to help you evaluate and get started on a path to resolution. Of course, it doesn't replace physiological and/or psychological assistance, which, as I've said before, I believe should also be a part of the process of looking for answers.

I also created this Guide as a resource for Spiritual Advocates. I believe it is the goal of a Spiritual Advocate to remain objective at all times, to refrain from making a decision about what's going on, and to provide education, information, and resources that will allow the person having the experiences to work towards their own resolution. This isn't to say that at some point intervention and assistance shouldn't be given. The question becomes when and how and in what form. As a Spiritual Advocate these lines can become blurred. We want to support and allow the belief in spirit activity and contact to be a possibility while also acknowledging that other causes may be at play. This Guide outlines an approach for considering each of these potential avenues.

Before we start to examine the actual activity in Chapter 2, I want to share the 5 Major Steps that need to always be applied when working through the identification and resolution process. I became aware of the importance of these when working with my own clients as well as those who contacted our paranormal group. They hold true no matter the outcome and actually apply to any challenging situation we may be enduring in life.

The 5 Major Steps for Resolving Spirit Activity

Step 1: Validate the Experience - It's important to note that in the perception of the one experiencing these events, (be that you or someone you're helping) the activity **IS** actually occurring. I didn't say why it's happening or even if it's real, only that it *is* happening. Don't devalue the experience, rather accept that it's a part of their/your current reality. As an Advocate, this requires support, care, and understanding for these events without us "deciding" for them what's happening. If you are the one having the experiences then allow yourself to recognize them as valid, even if you don't yet have all the answers. Don't label, just acknowledge and give yourself the freedom to feel and experience what's going on, which leads us to the next step.

Step 2: Remain Objective - Refrain from making a biased or belief-based decision until you've looked at all of the evidence and potential causes. If you believe in spirits and are inclined to view this as a potential reason, then ask yourself, "What else could be the cause?" And if you're a disbeliever, then you may want to also consider the question, "What if this is a spirit?" The goal is to remain open to both potentials so that you can look for answers and ways to move forward. The goal is not to reinforce your beliefs but rather to seek the truth.

If you're a Spiritual Advocate, then also refrain from taking a side. This is your key role for assisting someone having experiences. Help them to remain objective and consider a wide range of possibilities. When they feel unbalanced, be a stabilizing force until they feel capable of handling the decision-making process on their own

Step 3: Get Educated – I hate to say this, but sometimes we just don't want to spend the time to get the answers we need. We want a pill or a fast answer along with a prompt resolution. Or maybe we like to turn to others to solve our problems or make decisions for us. It's easier but it's not the way things work. Yes, we can and should seek out the wisdom and expertise of others, but they can't solve or decide for us what's happening in our lives. We have to be the one to educate ourselves and then make rational decisions that support our experiences.

If there's nothing going on then you need to know why, not take someone else's word for it. But if something is going on, then why trust anyone else to tell you what to believe? If real spirit activity is happening to you, then trust me, you'll run into plenty of people who won't support this decision. You can't let it undermine you. Get educated and make your own decisions!

If you're the Spiritual Advocate, then assist others in the educational process. You can do this by offering resources in the form of books, websites, and/or local support systems. You can also help them select relevant keywords and concepts to research and provide alternative potentials for their consideration. Your role is not only to bring information and insight, but to also encourage others to do their own research. Ensure they're working towards a solution and not relying on you to fix or resolve the matter for them.

Step 4: Seek Help When Needed – Don't be afraid to admit when things are beyond your ability to handle and you're in need of help. Know your limitations, especially if you're the Advocate, and know when to refer someone to another resource if you're unable to assist them.

If you are having the experiences, don't be afraid to admit you need help. This isn't always easy for most of us, as we're taught to be independent, self-reliant, and capable — but we all have our limits. There's no shame in needing help. It's how we grow!

Step 5: It's a Journey - Know that finding a resolution will be a process, whether or not the events are ultimately found to involve authentic spirit activity. If real spirit activity is occurring, then it's potentially going to cause a shift in your views and beliefs. Once the door is opened you can't return to your former way of living. Allow yourself the space to simply know that you're going to learn and understand more as time goes by.

If the spirit activity ends up not being real, then you have other questions to consider as a part of your journey. Is there a physiological or psychological issue that needs to be dealt with? Did you allow your fears and beliefs to take control? Do you feel a loss over the fact that there was no activity — or are you relieved? How has this event affected you, and how will it reshape your life and/or views? What have you learned, and/or what are you learning as a result of your experience?

Solutions and answers aren't found overnight, so be prepared for the resolution to take time and understand that the journey itself will offer many new, beneficial insights.

If you're a Spiritual Advocate, then you need to ensure the one having the experiences is actively seeking resolution and being accountable for the process. An Advocate can support and guide, but you may want to guard against the one having the experience becoming co-dependent and doing nothing about the matter. When you see this occurring, you may want to consider withdrawing assistance until you see action and progress on the part of the one having the experience.

In addition, as an Advocate, you need to know when your role is complete. During the journey process, you can't always be there every step of the way. Yes, you can be available for occasional questions and follow-up, but assisting someone for months is a long-term commitment you may not want to make unless the person you're assisting is an intimate loved one.

Summary: Looking for assistance and answers regarding spirit activity can be an overwhelming process, but it can also be a simple one if we remember the 5 Major Steps. With the extremes of skepticism and fear on one side of the spectrum to blind faith on the other, we can get lost when trying to understand something as mysterious as the world of spirits. Are they real? If they aren't, then what's happening to us? If they are, *then* what? There are plenty more questions to ask, so let's take a look at how we can start to identify real activity from false.

CHAPTER 2
IDENTIFYING FALSE SPIRIT ACTIVITY

There are six major causes for claims of spirit activity which end up being false or invalid. In this chapter, we will take a look at each of these causes individually.

Cause #1: Belief - The biggest culprit for false claims of spirit activity are personal beliefs. Beliefs are very powerful, but are not always accurate. Leaping to conclusions, making assumptions, and then labeling a so-called paranormal event as spirit-related is just not a grounded course of action. There's nothing wrong with allowing our experiences to convince us of newfound truths. However, openness to experience is different than making an uninformed assessment.

We need to remind ourselves that paranormal events can be caused by many things, some having nothing to do with spirit activity. If we can remain objective and look for a wide variety of potential explanations, then we're on the path to seeing if our beliefs have any credibility. Real spirit activity has discernible qualities that we should look for, and I'll discuss these in the next chapter.

Of course, another problem is that once we believe something to be true, there's very little that will convince us otherwise unless we allow new facts and awareness to replace the old assumptions. No one can do this work for you, although an Advocate may be able to help. In the end, developing the willingness to thoughtfully examine your beliefs is your responsibility. This doesn't mean that you must dismiss the activity as false, but it does mean letting go enough to be willing to consider other possibilities.

If we find we can't or won't let go of our belief in the activity, then we need to examine this as well. Does the experience fulfill a psychological need, or are we simply convinced to the point we won't budge? We are free to choose how we respond and what we believe, but recognize that if you or someone you are assisting is not willing to budge, then the only recourse is to move forward regarding the person's assumptions and/or refer them to someone else. If you are convinced but your Advocate is not, then the two of you will need to decide if you can continue to work together. There may be times when you'll need to seek help from other sources.

Cause #2: Environment - Strange activity can occur as a result of environmental factors. From time to time, electricity, magnetism, audio waves, water, minerals, and weather can all create unusual phenomena, and because we don't typically see or understand these forces, we may label them as paranormal or spirit-related. Balls of light may be a result of static electricity buildup and discharge. Mists may be a result of weather or gases. Tingling and hair raising may be due to power lines, electromagnetic fields (EMF), or other electrical influences. Just because we lack the ability to see or do not know the reason for certain events doesn't make them spirit-related.

So how can we tell if they're environmental?

Look for patterns in the events: note time of day, weather conditions, and other external indicators. If you live near industrial or commercial zones, such as businesses, arenas, or fire and police stations, realize that their operations could be affecting you or causing unusual activity. Airports, cell towers, power lines, military bases, and industrial plants can all have major impacts on our environment, so look to these as potential sources of activity, even if they're located many miles away. Weather patterns can carry smells, smokes, and gases miles from their sources, creating unsuspected effects. Knowing the industrial landscape around you can be very important in finding a potential cause.

If you feel comfortable, then ask your neighbors if they've noticed anything different or unusual. You don't have to say you think a spirit is involved. Just describe the feelings and events you're noticing and see if it fits for them as well. If multiple homes are noticing things, then this allows you to gather those clues and become better equipped for finding answers.

Do research to see if you can find other similar events or activities that fit your description, and then look for plausible explanations. Try to use reliable websites and people as resources while still allowing yourself to be both skeptic as well as believer. Scan the sites of skeptics, but also let yourself see what those who believe in spirit activity have to say. Many skeptics offer some very valid and potential insights regarding spirit or paranormal activity, so consider them; there's no harm in looking.

When doing research, you also need to realize that government, major industry, and big business are not always on the up and up about the truth. I'm not a conspiracy theorist by any means; however, some more controversial notions may be worth considering. For example, there's been a long debate about the effects of high voltage power lines on people, especially children. Some reports have claimed close proximity to these power lines may result in increased rates of childhood leukemia, cancer, and depression. At times, we have to ask what truths are being hidden for what some would consider the greater good — in this case, the ability for all people to have power.

A simple environmental cause many people overlook is animals. This may seem obvious, but we have to take into consideration how animals can burrow in, hunker down, and even reproduce within our living spaces. Young animals can make soft crying or mewing sounds that can be mistaken for voices, while larger animals can cause pipes to bang, walls to vibrate, and more.

Additional environmental causes also include tree branches or wires tapping or knocking against portions of the home as well as the rattling of loose housing materials. The expansion and contraction of building materials can also be a source of odd sounds. This can be caused by temperature and/or barometric changes. New construction, new surface materials, and even natural erosion and decay can all cause very normal parts of a home to suddenly give off an "activity" vibe. If sounds are the key complaint for your activity, then you need to do a thorough search for potential causes before assuming spirits are the source.

Creaking floorboards are also a common claim. People will often say they've never noticed the noise before, but this doesn't mean it wasn't there before. It simply means they've never acknowledged it and now that they have it's become quite obvious. This may sound absurd, but it's actually how the mind works. In other words, what was once an event that the subconscious mind packed away as inconsequential, the conscious mind has now acknowledged, resulting in greater recognition and notice. It seems new because suddenly it has relevance.

This type of subconscious/conscious recognition is especially heightened during times when the television is featuring paranormal "reality" shows (which I think by now most of us realize are not at all reality). When people watch these shows they start to "notice" things more because they are looking for them. As a result, their brain quite innocently seeks to fulfill their request and starts to notice what may have always been there.

It's important to note that activity with environmental causes is devoid of interaction. In other words, environmentally-caused events occur without intention, purpose or meaning. Now, they may very well have a pattern, especially if they're being triggered by something like business operations or other man-made physical forces. For example, the nearby lumber mill may run a large test every day at noon, causing our ears to ring even though we cannot hear the test. This pattern is discernible, but also devoid of interaction. We may give it meaning because we want it to be our dearly departed parents or the ghost of some tragic lost soul, but this doesn't make our suppositions true. While there are some spirit activities that do not "interact" and can parallel certain environmental phenomenon, we still need to evaluate the situations for all potential causes, not just one.

Cause #3: Physiological - When strange, unexplained things happen to our physical body sometimes we fear spirits may be the cause. However, physiological responses are sometimes at the root of seemingly ghostly experiences. Food and chemical sensitivities, sleep disorders, brain wave patterns, and our own brain's sensory processing can all create the illusion of a spirit's presence.

One physiological cause for false spirit activity can be sensitivity to food and other chemicals. Sugar is a common mind-altering substance that may lead to agitation and anger, and in some individuals, can even cause bad dreams. Drugs, alcohol and other chemicals may alter perceptions. While these substances may not cause problems for some people, they may be affecting you. Everyone has different tolerance levels and reactions to foods and chemicals, so it is important to know yourself and your body. If you're not physically healthy or are engaging in unhealthy habits, then this is always an area to review as a potential cause of so-called spirit activity. Even if your habits are long-standing, you may have reached a tipping point that has caused new side effects and experiences to develop.

It's very common for people to report spirit activity during the night, especially just upon waking or falling asleep. The sensation of being held down, touched, or spoken to can many times be explained by altered brainwave patterns and various sleep states, which can create a sense of "someone else" being around.

Sleep paralysis, for example, can be very frightening and has led to people believing they're being attacked. This condition causes people to temporarily experience an inability to move, speak, or react. Some people will conclude this is the result of a spirit attack. Once this fear takes hold and the belief sets in, it's extremely difficult to remove. The fear and stress combined with the physiological effects of sleep paralysis may falsely create a seeming barrage of negative spirit activity.

It's important to note that some people do experience spirit contact during sleep or just upon waking, especially during times of spiritual emergence (an intense time of spiritual awakening). However, valid spirit contact is typically positive, loving, and beneficial. If you are sensitive to spirit, you will most likely have a wide range of experiences — not just negative ones. If you're constantly fearful or convinced that negative spirits are around you, then you may want to consider some possible other causes before you assume spirit activity is the ultimate source.

Altered brain wave patterns and various sleep states truly need to be researched before seeking out spiritual assistance. There's a great deal of information available which can help us evaluate certain events more objectively. Key search words should include: Brain Wave States,

States of Consciousness, Sleep Disorders, Sleep Paralysis, and Out of Body Experiences. I also suggest that you do some research regarding consciousness and the brain, as well as consciousness and the mind. I've provided a list of Keywords in the Appendix to help you do some further research.

In addition to sleep states, another thing we need to study and understand is how we process information. Our brain and our mind have different functions. Our brain "creates" things and "makes" things happen because that's how it's designed to work. *Pareidolia* is the brain's way of making patterns and meaning out of sounds and images. For example, the brain wants us to believe that what we're seeing in the window is an evil face because that would give its shape meaning.

Our brain's task is to define, explain, and identify information in our environment, but it's up to our mind to decide what to do with this information. We get to choose what we do when we see that pattern of a face. If we buy into the visual, our emotions and thoughts will then support the identified pattern. This only reinforces the idea that what is happening is real, both to the mind and the brain. This reinforcement, however, does not make it true. Our perception became "real" because we saw a pattern and believed it to be true.

So how do we distinguish reality from *pareidolia* or our brain's ability to see faces in everything from toast to spaghetti to ink blots? Our perceptions can be false indicators that trick us into thinking something is there when it isn't. Our brain interprets sensory stimuli at the speed of light. Our senses were designed to keep us safe and alive, and they function rapidly in order to clue us in to potential threats in our surroundings. We need to be cognizant of how our brain observes and analyzes information before deciding what to do with it.

I do want to say, however, that just because all of these physiological causes can be identified, it does **not** mean that spirit activity is not happening. This is why an objective balance between belief and skepticism is a must. Conventional science argues that these events are a result of medical issues or natural bodily functions, and so they are. The larger question, however, is whether or not these causes are the source of the event or whether they give rise to and allow the event to take place. In other words, does the brain create the event or does it allow us to experience the event? Let me give you an example.

Out of Body Experiences (OBEs) can be duplicated in laboratory conditions. Because of this, one might consider them less than spiritual in nature and more of a medical matter. But if OBEs are merely a perception and not grounded in reality, what do we do with the knowledge that some OBE participants can see beyond walls, hear conversations in adjoining rooms, or retell facts they shouldn't know? Does the OBE, even though it was created medically, somehow allow the consciousness to escape the physical body? If so, how does it work and what does this say about our human potential?

This is an example of how discerning the line between physiological functions and the power of consciousness is not always as clear as everyone would like it to be. When we lack an explanation for something that seems to stretch that boundary of human potential, we tend to label it as spiritual and/or spirt-related. While OBEs themselves have nothing to do with spirit activity, they provide us with an example of an event that has both physiological and spiritual dimensions.

Examining these potential physiological causes will help us guard against mistaking a medical issue for spirit activity. By considering each in turn, we can set up proper controls and questions that can either validate or eliminate them as reasons for spirit activity.

Cause #4: Psychological - At times, psychological issues can also cause people to believe they're having very valid spirit-related experiences. Determining what is real and/or psychological is a very serious matter. On one hand, the skepticism of the modern medical community can create fear for those who feel they are having these issues. Fear of judgment, ridicule, or disbelief can cause people to avoid seeking psychological assistance. On the flip side, some Advocates may too freely believe in spirit activity and leap to the conclusion that something is spirit-related when in fact it is based in a psychological matter. Treading here can be dangerous for all involved: for the person experiencing the event, for the medical community treating it, and for the Spiritual Advocate who wishes to offer aide but realizes that a deeper issue may be at play.

The psychological reasons for experiencing false spirit activity differ in their source and degrees of intensity. Just because someone is having some psychological issues doesn't mean they're not a functioning adult or that they should be afraid. Anyone can have psychological issues of varying degrees, so we can't simply say that the presence of a psychological issue means someone is clinically affected. This would be like saying someone who has a sleep disorder is completely unhealthy. This is why seeking proper professional assessment and assistance needs to be an integral part of the identification process.

From my personal experience, I will say that people experiencing certain psychological issues in conjunction with claimed spirit activity, may misconstrue some events as spirit activity. They're usually deeply convinced the activity is real and often wishes them harm. Paranoia and intense stress may cause the individual to perceive the activity as constant or even following them everywhere they go.

In my experience, both as a Medium and through paranormal work, people experiencing clinical issues may be difficult to rationalize with and are best referred to a professional. They may be dead-set in their views and unwilling to consider alternative points of view. They will usually have long and arduous stories about everything the activity has done to them, perhaps even having things highly documented, filmed, or recorded. They usually want help with the situation, but will only seek out those who will support their beliefs and claims. Once they find such a person, these individuals may demand that the problem be fixed because they consider themselves powerless to do so. They tend to feel as if they are victims of their perceived reality and are unable to resolve the matter on their own.

For those who wish to offer help or are asked to give assistance, great care needs to be given when dealing with people in this state. It's wonderful to want to use our spiritual gifts to help others, but in a situation like this we need to encourage them to seek professional medical assistance. Seeking psychological help can be stressful for many reasons, including the fear of how one may be perceived. However, encouraging them to seek help gives them the opportunity to get the assistance they need, or at the very least, rule out any potential psychological causes.

As a Spiritual Advocate for others, my strong suggestion is that if you meet someone who may fall into this category you should promptly advise them to consider professional help. This is not easy as they are turning to you for spiritual help. You can be understanding and supportive, a listening ear for their woes, but overall, it's best not to advise or assist someone who is incapable of rational judgment regarding their experiences. This could spell disaster for you, personally as well as legally. Most Spiritual Advocates are not legally able to provide therapy or counseling. Those who are ordained can by law offer spiritual assistance, but they can still be held liable, so here again we need to be cautious.

If you're on the fence about whether or not you're having psychological issues, then there's no shame in seeking medical assistance or even spiritual assistance. You don't have to confess to belief in actual spirit activity to your medical professional, but you should describe your experiences in calmly, matter-of-factly, and detail. There may be some very simple medical issues that can be treated and which will help resolve the "activity." There is no shame in getting help. What matters is that you find the solutions you need to live a happy and successful life.

Psychosomatic issues should also be considered under the category of psychological causes. A psychosomatic issue is when people have experiences that seem valid and can even be witnessed by others, but are caused by the person themselves, not someone or something else. Mysterious scratches, hives, or welts may actually be the result of undocumented illness, environmental factors, or even disruptive, excess personal energy. When dealing with a potential psychosomatic issue, it's important to first rule out these other physical causes. If the issue is indeed psychosomatic, then symptoms may be caused by the individual unconsciously injuring themselves. Injury may be due to high levels of stress or belief in spirit involvement, whether spirit activity is real or not.

Some suspected spirit related issues may actually be created by an excess of personal energy. For instance, someone who is awakening to their awareness but is not sufficiently grounded may be vulnerable to disruptive energy much in the same way someone with a weakened immune system is vulnerable to illness. Granted, these cases are rare, but they can and do happen. Those who have psychosomatic symptoms and believe they are the result of spirit activity may be difficult to sway to a different perspective in part because their concern is rooted in fear.

In summing up the psychological cause, I have to urge caution, as sometimes valid negative spirit activity may be occurring. While we don't want to incite fear or encourage a belief in a false experience, we also don't want to discount a real experience that needs to be dealt with. This is the opposite of our role as an Advocate. If someone is claiming negative experiences, then we need to look at all the aforementioned clues and causes before we can validate true negative spirit activity. Determining the validity of spiritual activity is not easy, which is why many people seek help for these events. It's not easy for them either!

Cause #5: Self-Generated – This cause is a little deceptive, and in essence is fairly harmless, although it can certainly become a problem if not recognized and properly addressed. Self-generated activity is when we believe we're connecting with a spirit when we're not. How does this differ from belief? It differs because we believe we can converse with it, much as we would an imaginary friend.

I want to be careful here, as I firmly believe spirit communication is a real and viable skill; however, I also believe it's not as common as some people make it out to be. I talk more about true spirit activity in Chapter 3, so for now let's address why this communication could be misleading.

Much as children do when playing with a make-believe friend, we as adults can allow our inner dialogue, imagination, and subconscious thoughts to play into the notion of real spirit communication. This is very common in people who are starting to have emerging psychic or mediumship abilities; however, the existence of psychic abilities does not mean all experiences are valid. It can be very tough to discern actual spirit communication from that of self-generated communication, which is why we need to consider this as a real possibility for claimed activity.

So, how do we resolve this?

Typically, there needs to be some form of validation involved in order to help the person with the experience discern if what's happening is valid or self-generated. Many parents dismiss the notion of children communicating with spirits as nothing more than imagination. Sometimes it is. However, if a child can describe someone you know, provide specific details about their life, and share personal information, then this may not be self-generated, but in fact communication with an actual spirit person.

During my own personal psychic opening, which I talk about in my book *Surviving Spiritual Emergence,* I also had to come to terms with what was happening, and the only way I could do this was to gain validation for my emerging awareness. This was done by seeking out ways to utilize this internally received information for others. Only by exploring it could I begin to discern the varying levels of awareness and to understand those that were self-generated from those that were valid. In other words, we learn by doing.

If you're having conversations with spirits and this is resulting in some form of activity for you, then you need to seek validation for your thoughts. If not, you'll never be certain if your communications are genuine. This can lead you down a path of self-deception. To find validation, engage in intuitive or psychic support groups or classes. Practice on your friends. Ask the spirits for information you can validate or verify through research. All of these will help you to distinguish valid communication and avoid self-generated interactions.

In some instances, people may be quite convinced their awareness of spirits is based on actual contact and activity, perhaps even considering themselves a psychic or a medium. However, when the time comes to provide validation for their thoughts, the facts and details may be inaccurate. Individuals who fail to gain accurate validation may stick to sharing broader messages that are positive and uplifting, though general in nature.

Now is there any harm being done here?

Some might say "yes" when someone has paid for psychic or mediumship services. However, there is typically no intent to harm or deceive because in the mind of the practitioner, the spirit interaction is genuine. This is vastly different from what I call the dime-store psychics who know full well all they have to do is throw out some general fluff to make a buck. Their intent is vastly different from those described above.

This type of self-generated internal awareness and dialogue can lead some people to be convinced spirit activity is real. There's nothing wrong with this as it's a normal phase of true psychic opening. However, a Spiritual Advocate should encourage such people to get training, education, and work with others to validate their awareness to ensure it's real.

In addition, self-generated information may be helpful and kind or negative and frightening. It's very important to also note that this may NOT be a result of psychological issues. It's really just a misguided belief, where the lines of fantasy and reality have blurred and yet the ability to function is still present.

Cause #6: Human Intervention – This may seem a bit of an obvious cause, but there are times when actual living people are the cause of so-called spirit activity. Human intervention may be perfectly innocent — or deliberate and perhaps even malicious. For example, if things end up missing and then reappearing, we have to consider other housemates as potential causes. This has been true in several cases where clients were claiming items were disappearing in their home. When asked about housemates, they truly may not have considered this as a possibility. Since the items in question were often borrowed one day and then returned to their same location the next, many simply assumed spirit intervention. Now, of course, this isn't to say there wasn't spirit activity, but we need to consider the obvious before moving on to spirits as the cause.

There are also some people who fake and/or stage activity for their own benefit or gain. It's rare, but it does happen, so we need to be sure to consider the fact that the one claiming the activity may have ulterior motives. These folks tend to enjoy the attention and will want you to "confirm" for them what's going on, as if getting you to cast your vote will support their agenda (whatever that may be).

And finally, there are those times when someone is pulling a prank, trying to convince an Advocate or someone else that activity is occurring when it isn't. They're not looking for fame and fortune, but instead want to poke fun. They may even want someone to confirm the activity so they can be the one to prove the event was staged.

If you're someone experiencing activity, then don't forget to look at other people as an obvious source. If it's a prank, try not to react or get flustered. That may be what someone is looking for. If you suspect other people, then ask them, but realize they may deny involvement if they have their own agenda. Try to set up conditions that could eliminate people as the potential problem, or in a worst-cased scenario, set up a hidden camera in areas where things are happening.

If you're an Advocate assisting someone, then don't miss this critical potential cause. Your reputation could be on the line if you claim valid spirit activity and it ends up being a result of others, whether or not they were deliberately faking the activity. Remember to simply lay out the potential causes and remain objective. Your clients have to discover the truth for themselves, but be certain you and they consider this option before making a final claim of real spirit activity.

The Orb Controversy – Orbs, orbs, and more orbs. I must confess right out of the gate that I'm highly skeptical of these as actual spirit activity, which is why I have placed them under the category of identifying false spirit activity. However, I know many people who are deep believers. For this reason, I tend to steer clear of this discussion when it comes to orbs as spirits.

It's important to note that I've seen strange light ball phenomenon with my own eyes. The color and intensity of this light is more like lightening and nothing like car lights or other man-made electrical sources. It has an intensity and clarity that is deeply unique, but does this make it spirit-related? This reminds me of those movies where time travelers hand a flashlight to some indigenous tribe and they see them as gods for creating light. Just because we don't understand what it is or how it's done doesn't make it spirit-related. Granted, it doesn't mean it's **not** spirit activity, but how can we tell? It's just not that simple, and we need to examine a wide range of potential causes before leaping to a spirit-based conclusion.

Cameras and other image-capturing devices are simply unreliable. The mere presence of the lens itself creates a refractory state that can allow for odd occurrences in photos, including not only orbs but also streaks, shadows, and other plays of light. Even infrared cameras reflect off bugs, dust, and other particulate matter which seemingly floats with intelligence and yet is most often blown aloft by air currents we can't see or even feel. Nothing around us is ever static.

There are people who study orb activity and swear by it, so I would encourage you to find them for an opposing view. Just remember, even if we don't use a flash on our photo device, there are still internal lighting and lenses which can create effects that will only be seen on the end result.

Summary: As we can see from these six causes, the biggest reason for claims of false spirit activity is a lack of objectivity. It's natural to need to understand and then rush to define our experiences, but we must consider numerous possibilities before reaching a final conclusion. This is why objectivity is our biggest friend when searching for answers.

As you go about looking for answers, allow yourself to remain open enough to consider and explore each of the above areas. Think of yourself as Sherlock Holmes and seek out the logical causes. If you need someone to do this for you, then look for help both in the medical as well as spiritual fields. Remember, your main objective is to find the truth, and you can only do this by considering all the possible alternatives before reaching a final conclusion.

CHAPTER 3
IDENTIFYING TRUE SPIRIT ACTIVITY

How can we identify true spirit activity? This depends on how we are experiencing it. There are two ways this can happen: one is to **observe** it and the other is to be **aware** of it.

When we **observe** true spirit activity we'll recognize it in our physical environment. We may catch a glimpse of a shadow or a slight smell. Lights act funny or things go missing then reappear. The picture frame always ends up face down, doors close on their own and floors creak, or we hear footsteps. As a result, **observation** is when we recognize there's a disruption in the physical environment which causes us to take notice.

Awareness, on the other hand, is when we sense the presence of spirits rather than observe them. We may get a funny feeling or the hair on our arm rises. Perhaps we feel electrified or as if someone is standing near us. We may get an internal knowing of thoughts, feelings or even words that seemingly do not belong to us. In other words, what's happening is occurring internally rather than externally.

Before we can start to identify the potential source of activity, we need to discern which of the above two scenarios are at play. Either one or the other may be occurring — or even both. Every situation is unique.

I want to add a word of caution here for those working with a paranormal group. Many groups are seeking **observational** cases where some form of proof lies in the physical environment. But what about those people who are having an **awareness** of activity rather than an **observation**? An investigation will most likely yield no results since nothing physical was happening anyway. This can be disconcerting for all involved, especially if the group itself is highly skeptical or biased regarding their belief in spirits in general. This is why understanding the two potential sources of spirit activity are important.

We've already discussed some potential causes for false spirit activity. If the activity is real, we already know the cause: a spirit. As a result, we don't need to examine the actual cause, but rather seek to ensure it really is a spirit.

Let's begin with some things to look for when activity is occurring based on external events and our **observation** of them.

Observation #1: Interaction − While this is not 100% true in every case, a majority of the time true spirit activity is interactive in nature. Think of it this way: someone who loves and cares about you and is in spirit wants your attention. How are they going to get it? Most typically by trying to strongly affect your surroundings. This can happen through signs and other simple ways or it can happen in more drastic ways such as affecting the environment around you.

If this is the case, then we need to look for interactive qualities. Does it respond when we ask it to? Does it happen at certain important or significant times? Does it seem to have some form of intelligence behind it?

Now, I know this can be tough to discern. For example, lighting could be going bad, new patterns of light and shadows could be from cars or newly cleared land, or camera and photography lighting could cause orbs. There are many physical explanations we need to consider before jumping to a final conclusion. If, however, the spirit of a loved one is around, then they'll know this and will look for a loving and interactive way to get your attention

What happens if the event never repeats itself? Does this make it a coincidence or false activity since it wasn't interactive? Activity will not always continue on a regular basis, and therefore, interaction may not occur. The activity may be a one-time event designed to get your attention. This leads us to our next observation, that of timing.

Observation #2: Timing – I mentioned timing under physical causes, but timing can also be a validating factor for true spirit activity. The example of the lumber mill test happening every day at noon is an event which occurs at an exact time and repeats itself. This timed repetition suggests physical causes, but true spirit activity can also having timing. The difference is that the timing of spirit activity is usually focused around you and your life, rather than a specific time of day. Here's an example.

You're washing dishes and thinking about the best friend you have just lost. It's only been a few weeks, but you miss her terribly. As you think of her and begin to cry, the lights flicker for just a brief moment. You observe there's no wind or foul weather which could be affecting the power and this has never happened before, so you note the odd timing of the event. Of course, this is not to say the activity is valid; however, the timing as it personally relates to you is worth noting.

It's important to note thoughts, feelings, and even special events (birthdays, weddings, etc.) when potential spirt-related activities occur. Their correlation to other happenings in your personal life is the type of timing issue you'll want to look for. When activity coincides with life events, it lends credence to the idea that the activity may be spirit related.

Observation #3: Persistence – As with timing, persistent activity can also be the result of physical causes, most especially when the activity occurs at predictable times. For example, if the lumber mill test is run seven days a week and always at noon, the activity will show persistent timing and be the result of a physical cause.

In cases of valid spirit activity, the persistence may remain but its style, type, and frequency will tend to vary. In other words, one day the lights may flicker and the next day your keys end up missing from the hook on the wall only to mysteriously reappear an hour later (with no human intervention). Or perhaps you hear noises at various times of the day. All of this activity is persistent but not consistent: a big indicator that something else might be going on.

Observation #4: Echoes, Imprints, & Residuals – I want to spend a moment and talk about valid spirit activity that we can observe, but which does not fall into the aforementioned observations. These are often referred to as residuals, imprints, and/or echoes. This is when the activity from a place and/or a different time period is overlapping and affecting the current location. Common examples include land that may have had high levels of human activity on it, historical locations with past high energy/emotional events, or buildings with high levels of human interaction.

In each of these cases, spirit activity may be observed; however, it is not actually interacting or designed to affect the people who experience it. It's merely as its name suggests, an echo of a time past. And if we want to get even more technical, since all time is simultaneous, the events are actually still going on, but I won't get into that here.

So why do these events occur?

Typically, there was some historical or energetic connection tied to the location, and for some unexplained reason this activity bleeds through so that we humans can perceive it. It's important to note that this does not mean an actual spirit is haunting the place. It merely means that for some unknown reason, the events of the past are seeping into our time. Though we can observe them and they are valid spirit activity, an actual spirit itself is not causing the events to happen. An imprint will lack interaction and responsiveness, although it may have timing and be persistent. Let me give you a good example of what I mean.

There's an old building that's been around since the turn of the century. Today it's a restaurant, but at the turn of the century it was a tavern which hosted large parties and dancing girls. Patrons dining will often report hearing piano music, especially in the evenings. The staff replies this is quite common and many people hear it. They also explain the building's history as a dance hall and saloon as the suspected cause of the music. Now some people might use this example to say a ghost is playing the music. That may be true, but it may merely be an echo or an imprint of those past events.

It's important to make note of this type of activity if you feel you're commonly hearing footsteps, laughter, or other odd sounds. The activity may have nothing to do with you personally. It may simply be happening and you're observing it. Of course, defining if it's an imprint/echo or the actual presence of a spirit can be tough to discern; remember, if the activity is interactive, it's most likely created by the actual presence of someone.

Now that we've reviewed how to determine if *observable* activity is valid, we will review how to determine the validity of spirit activity we are *aware* of. This type of activity can be quite different in that there may actually be nothing happening in the environment, yet we sense the presence of spirits internally.

Awareness #1: Awareness – This may seem a bit redundant, but the largest difference between observable spirit activity and the awareness of it, *is*, in fact, our *awareness*. In other words, there is a sensation or sense that someone is present, even though there is no observable physical phenomenon in the environment to support that claim. It's purely an internal experience.

How this manifests is very unique to each person. It tends to also be more observable in children, as they have not yet learned that awareness of spirits is considered "impossible" or "wrong." They will hear spirits, be aware of them, and may even converse with them and know certain facts about their lives. Of course, the same can be true for adults as well, but children are more commonly receptive to spirit activity via awareness than adults.

For people born with the awareness of spirits, depending on whether or not they embraced or rejected the awareness, spirit activity may be a way of life; while for others the awareness may emerge later in life and require a period of adjustment. When this awareness emerges later in life, it tends to be rather unsettling.

In the case of spirit awareness, we must be sure to consider and eliminate potential physiological or psychological causes. If we have genuine spirit awareness, commonly referred to as being psychic and/or a medium, our awareness needs to be grounded in reality. We need to work with the awareness so that we can discern real spirit activity from false. Surprisingly enough, many people who were born with this ability push it aside out of fear and judgment. So while they may have awareness, they may also have repressed it and/or have spent little time learning about it, how it works, or what to do with it.

Awareness #2: Interactive – As with observation, interaction will also occur with an awareness of spirit activity. In other words, the activity will interact with us, although the interaction will be quite different when it's internal vs. external. At an internal level we may hear words, know thoughts, get feelings or sensations, feel our body is affected, or get flashes of images. But no matter how these internal clues occur, they're still interactive in that we can converse with them and receive answers.

Awareness #3: Verifiable – Determining fantasy from reality is critical when dealing with true spirit activity that is the result of our awareness. The **ONLY** way this can happen is by verifying its presence, but how do we do this?

We ask for proof!

When our awareness puts us in connection with a spirit, we need to be able to validate and verify their presence. By asking the spirit to give us information and send some form of validation that they're real, we look for assistance from them to verify their existence. Of course, we tend to look for a big, earth-shattering, physical experience, but most validating experiences are more subtle and tend to happen internally. If our awareness of spirit is internal, then most likely the reply will also be internal. We can ask for an external response which is observable, but the response tends to come in the form of signs, patterns, and sometimes from other people rather than in flickering bulbs or blurry shadows. Why? Because it's far easier for spirits to connect with the heart and mind than it is for them to affect physical matter.

Common questions to ask a spirit are to have them tell you something or show you something of importance. I recall on one occasion I needed validation regarding a matter, and I heard in my head the word "rhinoceros." It was a bit odd, and something I thought I would never see living where I do in the Pacific Northwest. Within a week's time, however, I ran into a rhinoceros, not once, but three times — and all on the same day! (They were not real, by the way, but works of art and pictures). After that, I didn't see rhinoceroses anymore, and I took this as clear validation regarding my exchange with the spirit.

Another way to validate your awareness is to start to use it around and with other people. This is an immensely frightening experience for many. Gaining the courage to validate the awareness of a spirit with others is truly a leap of faith — believe me, I know! But it's also a sure-fire way to ensure your awareness is accurate and not self-generated or false.

Summary: To ensure our awareness of spirits is real, we should determine if the characteristics mentioned in this chapter are present. Valid spirit activity is often verifiable and interactive. Awareness of spirit activity crosses into the realm of psychic awareness and mediumship. We are not able to fully explore those topics here, but if you suspect your awareness is the source of the spirit activity, then I strongly encourage expanding your education in these fields to gain a greater understanding of the events happening to you.

To fully explore spirit activity with observable effects, we need to allow time to pass and to continue to observe the events. The suggestions in this chapter are brief, but if you work with them in conjunction with the physical causes in chapter two, you will start to find better answers. In other words, by eliminating potential physical causes, we are left with only the spirit-based ones. When determining the nature of spirit-based activity, look for interaction as well as timing and persistence, while remembering that an echo or imprint could be a potential cause.

CHAPTER 4
DEALING WITH FEAR

Spirit activity, real or otherwise, elicits so much fear. Above all else, this has been the most common reaction I've seen from people. During my own experiences and exploration I found it all rather fascinating, but perhaps this was because my interactions were all positive, supportive, and uplifting. I wasn't seeking spirit activity; it simply happened to me and came in the form of awareness, and was all positive and loving. As a result, I embraced the journey.

Of course, not everyone feels the same way. While the origin of people's fears varies, I believe that Hollywood and religion are the two biggest culprits. I know this opinion may not make me popular, but this truly has been the case for most of the people I've worked with. I don't want to address these sources or place blame, but rather deal with the fear itself. No matter what causes it, the fear is really the issue, so this is what we need to examine.

Above all else, fear creates an emotional imbalance that makes objectivity difficult and thus impedes resolution. Sometimes people get so stuck in the fear of what's happening they can't even think straight. They aren't crazy or mentally disturbed, rather the emotional upheaval has become so over-powering that finding their center is tough. As a result, people look for help, and the kind of help they seek will depend on their version of what's happening. If they believe spirit activity is the cause, then they'll seek out those they feel can understand these experiences: this puts us back to square one, or in this case, Chapter 1, where I address how to start the process.

The biggest suggestion I can make to people is to keep the fear at bay. Often we leap to conclusions about spirit activity, real or otherwise, and make assumptions about it. The fact is, if we're having spirit activity and we're not used to it, then how much can we really know about it? This lack of knowledge combined with misinformation from other sources creates a dynamic that might be impossible to escape, and more importantly, may be entirely false. In other words, the activity may be completely harmless and benign; we've simply reacted with misplaced fear.

Of course, I realize that it's easy for me to sit in my office and write about remaining calm. However, I understand this isn't always so easy to do, especially if we perceive our experiences with the activity as negative. Still, somewhere along the way we have to find the courage and wherewithal to look at our emotional issues objectively.

So what are some steps to help us do this?

Fear-Buster #1: Admit You Don't Know the Cause of What's Going On - The truth is, when spirit activity begins to occur, we don't really know the cause right away. You may have some ideas and will leap to some conclusions, but by admitting that you truly don't know what's happening yet, you can begin to look at the situation objectively.

Fear-Buster #2: Commit to Finding Answers & Know They're Out There – Empower yourself by realizing the answers you need are out there — and commit to getting them. You may not know what to do at this very moment because the experience is new, but I can assure you other people have gone through this. Luckily, we live in a country where people can freely express their views and experiences. We also live in a day and age where information is only a mouse-click away. Don't allow yourself to feel disempowered because you don't know what to do. The experience is new and foreign, nothing more. You can and will find the answers. It just takes a little work and commitment.

Fear-Buster #3: Recognize You Don't Know Why the Activity Is Occurring – In Fear-Buster #1 I refer to the fact that you don't know a *cause* for the activity. With this fear-buster I'm referring to your not knowing *why* it's happening, which is very different from knowing its cause. Let me explain.

If the evaluation process reveals that the activity is valid, then we have to admit that as of yet we don't know why it's happening. "Why me?" This is a big question that everyone asks. And it's a very good question which I address in Chapter 6. However, the answer varies with the situation, and you will need to spend some time to figure that out.

Is the activity tied to a place or the land? Is it a result of you or someone in the home? Is it a result of someone reaching out to you, or are you simply becoming more aware? Is it a result of your neighbors, or is it simply a random event?

The truth is, you don't know why the activity is occurring. Many people leap to a conclusion and internalize the experience, assuming it's all about them. Maybe it is, but then again, maybe it isn't. Try to keep your fear at bay by realizing you don't really know why the event is happening, at least not yet.

Fear-Buster #4: Spirits Are People — Both Good & Bad, But Mainly Good – It's funny how often activity conjures up visions of evil spirits or tortured souls who somehow want to do us harm. Again, I think this is a fear response generated by outside sources, because until now, this misinformation is all we've known. However, spirits are just people. Most of them are good-hearted and kind and just going about doing their own thing. Their goal isn't to hurt, harm, or scare you. It's just to make contact. It's our reaction which creates the fear — not their actual presence, but time and time again, I see people immediately conclude that any and/or all contact is bad.

Unless something truly harmful has happened to you, which again is quite rare, then ask yourself: is anything scary really happening, or are you simply being fearful of the unknown? Is it your preconceived idea that spirits are 'bad' which is causing you to be fearful?

Now I know that many people say to be cautious when dealing with the spirit world, that all spirit activity is about deception. I can understand this fear, but again I have to counter with the argument that if bad spirits exist, then there must also be good ones. And wouldn't good spirits also want to be a part of our lives and to help us in life?

I think caution is certainly understandable; however, one way to conquer fear is to recognize that there are good spirits out there, just as there are good people, and they far outnumber the bad folks.

Fear-Buster #5: You Are Not a Powerless Victim – It's funny how much power we allow the spirit world to have over the physical. It's as if we think only bad people make contact, and that then when they do, they have total control of us and our world. How could that happen — and why would we think that?

You are not a victim, you are not powerless, and this is our world. We have nothing to fear except fear itself. How true this adage really is! Fear is what allows the power to exist in the first place. You are every bit as important, valuable, and powerful as those in spirit. You are born from the Source, from God: therefore, the spirits have no more power over you other than what you give them, and you only give them power when you fear.

While we fear what we don't understand, this does not make spirits more powerful than us. You are here on purpose, with the same power within your consciousness as in the entire Universe. That makes you a viable powerhouse of will, intention, energy, and emotion. No one can take any of that from you, not even spirits. The fact that you **think** they can is where their power lies, so why give it away? Some spirits may take advantage of this fact, however most will not. And this wisdom holds true for people in this world as well! It's sound advice for dealing with all people, both physical and spiritual.

If you're feeling powerless or helpless, then there's more than likely some kind of belief you're harboring which is contributing to that notion. You may need some deep introspection and evaluation to reclaim your true power, and unless you do, you may continue to experience fear until you give yourself permission to rise above it. You may also find that this sense of powerlessness exists in your real world as well or at some deeper inner level. So if nothing else, this may be an opportunity to ask yourself why you feel powerless against some spirit which in truth has no power over you other than what you give it.

Summary: Removing fear is probably the single most empowering thing you can do for yourself. Whether the activity is true or false, we rarely will come to rational decisions when plagued with this emotion. Our mind and body react to fear with the proverbial flight or fight response. This shuts down our rational processes and sends us into emotional overdrive. Do your best to realize you still lack a lot of answers, but have the ability and personal power to resolve them in the days ahead!

CHAPTER 5
NEGATIVE EXPERIENCES

I can't in all good conscience write about spirit activity and not address negative experiences. Just as in real life, while most people mind their own business, there are those few who aim to harass and upset the lives of others, for reasons only they know or understand. However, I want to be clear that in the majority of cases I've seen, a negative spirit experience is a matter of perception. In other words, when that good old fear sets in, we believe things are bad or negative whether they really are or not. Old programming, current beliefs, and personal ideologies can also cause us to fear unnecessarily.

So what defines true negative experiences? Let's first take a look at some common complaints regarding negative experiences.

Complaint #1: The Activity Is Scary and/or Scaring Me/Us – Some people will say that a spirit is scaring them or their children. If this describes your situation, ask yourself: is the spirit causing fear — or am I? How you react to spirt activity can cause those who turn to you for guidance to react in similar fashion. If you're scared, then ask yourself why. Is it because the experience is new, because you fear harm, or because you don't understand what is happening? If you believe the spirit is trying to scare you, ask yourself exactly how they are doing this. What part of the actual activity (excluding the presence itself) can be defined as scary? Be aware of the dialogue in your head about spirits and spirit activity. Do you believe all spirit activity and/or communication is wrong, evil, and caused by demons? If so, then your beliefs could be the sole basis of your fear and the reason you're labeling the experience as negative.

Try to evaluate why you're afraid and why you're labeling the activity as negative. Make a specific list of events without adding any emotional content. If you're unable to remain objective, please find someone who can review your list with you to see if they feel the activity is truly trying to scare you or if you're simply reacting with fear.

If the activity is in fact working to scare you, then you'll want to clearly understand why. This information will be helpful in resolving the issue.

Complaint #2: The Activity Is Harassing Me/Us – Like the above complaint, some people will say they're being harassed. Again, we have to ask what harassment involves. If the reply is only that the spirit is present all the time, then is this really harassment? Granted, we may find it distracting, disruptive, or even annoying, but to say they're "harassing" us may be a stretch, especially if the activity is based on an echo/imprint. Create an objective list of the exact activity, including specific examples of events that bothered you, before you label it as harassment. Make note of why you feel harassed so that you can clearly see why the activity is bothering you.

Complaint #3: I'm Being Attacked – This is a far more serious complaint than the previous two. When someone claims they are being attacked, we have to ask what this means and then discern whether or not the attack is physical, emotional, or mental.

Physical attacks are when some part of the physical being is affected. This may include feeling pushed, pinched, scratched; experiencing nausea or pain; or having some part of the body or clothing pulled. In other words, the spirit is imposing itself upon us in a physical way.

Remember that sleep-related issues can result in claims of physical attacks. If someone indicates they're being held down at night, feeling pressure on their body or chest, and/or can't move upon waking, then you may want to consider sleep paralysis and/or sleep apnea as potential causes.

Some people also claim sexual violation. Sexual experiences are quite common during sleeping states, so be sure to clarify when the event is taking place. Both men and women can have nocturnal orgasms that may be falsely considered spirit violation.

If you're someone experiencing physical attacks, then do your best to document what's happening: note time of day, location, as well as what you were doing, thinking, and feeling. If other people are in the home, then make note of this as well. If someone was present for the event, then ask them to also note what they saw.

Photos, video, and audio can all be very helpful if you plan on seeking assistance from others. However, these can be altered and/or faked, so expect skepticism, but document as much as you can anyway. If the events are recurring, plan ahead. It can be tough to think about documenting initially after an attack. The events can be emotionally jarring in every way, and sometimes the last thing you're thinking about is getting a photo or video. By being prepared, you are more likely to capture evidence.

I want to add something important about documenting, and that's not to get obsessed with it. Don't let it overtake your life or become all you think about. If the events truly are founded on actual spirit activity with negative intent, then by paying such close attention to them you're actually feeding the very thing you wish to avoid. Think of it this way: the spirit activity is like a kid who wants your attention, and the more attention you give, the harder it is to get away. They just keep wanting more and more. You're the one who sets the boundaries. Simply note the events and then do your best to go on about your day.

Emotional attacks are much harder to detect and almost impossible to determine or validate. As they can only be perceived with awareness, you'll most likely have to really work to discern what's going on by examining events over time and with diligence. Rarely will someone truly be able to help you discover if these attacks are real or imagined. However, this does not mean there's no help or hope available.

Emotional attacks will typically leave you drained and may include bouts of sadness, depression, anger, rage, or a wide variety of other negative feelings. I cannot stress enough that every effort must be made to seek professional medical help regarding these symptoms. Leaping to the conclusion of negative feelings being solely spirit-related is not a balanced point of view, and real or imagined, believing any spirit has this kind of power over you is not the way to resolve it. Serious health issues may very well be at play, so please seek medical assistance before assuming a spirit is attacking you.

There are also living people out there who claim to be "energy vampires." They state that they can utilize and take the energy of others for their own use. Is this real or not? I suppose it depends on your personal point of view. I've also run into a few cases where people have claimed to feel cursed or attacked from living people who were trying to negatively affect their lives. These claimed attacks have been real to them, so we may need to consider the possibility of someone living intending us energetic harm. We might ask ourselves: Do we have enemies or know of people who may wish us harm?

On the other hand, we also need to realize that a bad run of luck doesn't mean someone has "cursed us" or is sucking away our life force energy. Bad things happen, but so do good things. Are we looking at our blessings or only our disasters? Are we being accountable for the bad things in our lives? In other words, do we acknowledge how we created those situations for ourselves? We have to be accountable for our own emotional state before we can clearly recognize if someone else, living or otherwise, may be the actual cause.

Like emotional attacks, **mental attacks** are internal and therefore a matter of awareness. Here again, we need objectivity and to seek medical assistance before assuming spirits are to blame. Mental attacks may cause us to feel someone is always trying to contact us, invading our mental space, or is even poking at our brain. We may hear a singular persistent voice or perhaps many voices. These voices may engage in a negative and/or highly abusive dialogue.

One way to help you discern mental and emotional attacks is to recognize that they will tend to be incongruent with your current state of being; in other words, you may be happy and joyous when all of a sudden you feel an overwhelming sense of sadness or anger. We need to rule out disorders like bipolar spectrum disorders or dissociative identity disorder (multiple personality disorder) before we leap to this conclusion. Keeping track of the events in a journal will not only help a Spiritual Advocate in their assistance with you, but more importantly, will also help the medical community.

I also want to mention again psychosomatic causes as a reason people may perceive themselves as being attacked. I believe true negative experiences are rare, but when we strongly believe something is true, even when it's not, it may actually start to materialize. In these cases, the effects are of our own doing and not because of an actual spirit. In essence, we've "believed" ourselves into thinking something is true to the point that it starts to actually become true, but it's still not real. It's much like the placebo effect!

Complaint #4: I Saw an Evil Spirit in the Window (Or in Something Else) – As I said in Chapter 2, the brain can rapidly identify faces and images, so we need to look carefully to discover if an event of this description is based on actual spirit activity or something more plausible. I've had people swear that the face of a demon was carved into their bedroom door or peering through a window, and when shown, I was in fact able to see what they saw. Of course, when alternative options were provided, most people were still quite convinced that the presence was real.

There is little rationale one can provide in the face of this firm belief. After all, you can see it! Of course, you could ask: Why would the spirit of a demon be trapped in a door in your house? And if it is, is anything happening because of it, or do you just see it?

Faced with a lack of concrete answers to these questions, some people may be prompted to consider explanations that are more rational. However, others will find ways to reinforce their belief.

In situations like this one, people are really looking for validation and support for their conclusions, not an objective answer. When offered an opposing view, these types of folks typically will not contact you or speak to you again, no doubt already looking for someone who will agree with them. Their minds are already made up, so in essence they really weren't looking for assistance, simply validation, which is not the role of a Spiritual Advocate.

Pareidolia is the leading cause of "seeing" things in objects and photos. We'd all like to visually see something in order to help us prove spirits are real, but we also need to avoid looking for patterns and making things fit. If I saw a flower or a butterfly in a wisp of smoke, does that mean the butterfly or flower is real? Does it make it a spirit butterfly or a spirit flower? Or is it merely an identifiable pattern? Most likely it's the latter.

Some of my colleagues might consider this view harsh and may argue that a spirit could have created an image as a sign to show us they are present. The answer is: Maybe they did or maybe they didn't. Signs differ from random, singular events; they typically exhibit unusual patterns and timing and create great impact.

So, while we each get to choose what we see and what we believe, we should also be cautious in saying we know for sure. Sometimes the signs may have significance, while at other times they may be nothing at all.

Correlation is also an important part of validating actual spirit-related activity. If a butterfly is a sign you feel is associated with your departed father, and you see a butterfly in a picture, then you might wonder, "Was it dad?" A great way to validate the sign would be to ask dad to do it again; the repetition of the event lends more credibility to its occurrence. Or you can ask dad to send you a butterfly in a new way.

So while we may see the face of Mother Mary in a piece of toast, we have to ask if it's actually a message from Mother Mary herself, if it's a spiritual sign or clue, or if it's simply a case of pareidolia. In the end, we'll all assign meaning based on our views and beliefs, but if you're afraid of a demon or evil spirit, then I have to say the last thing you want to do it is give it any more power by acknowledging it as real. Laugh it off as a funny pattern you've observed and then move on. We'd be far wiser and safer looking for butterflies and flowers than demons and evil spirits.

Complaint #5: I'm Being Haunted - Typically this refers to the fact that someone feels a spirit is following them around **and** that it's less than friendly. As a Medium I'm often aware of spirits, and like living people, each one is different. However, I don't feel haunted any more than I would feel threatened if a stranger on the street approached me. Whether we feel threatened by strangers on the street depends on the circumstances and to some extent, our personalities. The same is true of our reaction to spirits. If you are on guard around strangers, then you'll most likely respond the same way towards spirits. It just comes down to who we are.

The big question regarding feeling "haunted" is whether or not the activity is causing you harm. The activity may cause you to wonder who it is and why it is approaching you, and may even leave you a little unsettled. However, rather than being a harmful spirit, couldn't it instead be someone who loves and cares about you? Why do you assume it's "haunting" you and that it's negative? These are all questions we need to consider when feeling haunted. And of course we need to consider any potential physiological or psychological causes.

Spirits have a life to live. They're just doing it somewhere else, but from time to time, they call on us, and from time to time, some do hang out closer to the earthly world. If you're feeling haunted ALL the time, then I would ask you to consider some possible alternatives. This is not to say the spirits of others aren't around us and often felt, but they also have their own lives to live and are not out to haunt or follow us every minute of the day. If you're feeling a persistent nagging about a spirit, then you'll want to rule out any physiological or psychological causes first, and then consider spirit contact as a last resort.

Should an actual spirit end up being the true cause, then trying to discover why the spirit is with you should be your first goal. To fear it doesn't help resolve the matter, only hinders your finding a resolution. Do some evaluating to determine if the spirit wants something and if you can be of help. If not, then you need to send them on their way.

Demons & Non-Human Beings – I plan to spend little time on this topic as I have no desire or interest in giving these types of experiences any of my energy or focus. Do I believe in them? I'm not sure, but then again I don't want to know.

If my goal is to maintain a spiritually strong self, then why does knowing this even matter? And, if I think I see or encounter such a thing, then why would I react with fear or even pursue it? This is not the correct course of action. Personally, I would completely dismiss it and go about focusing my energy on those spirits who love and support me. I give no thought or energy to these things because I choose not to. As a result, I don't plan to address the matter.

If you are looking for more exact answers regarding these questions, then I would urge you to do so carefully and only if you are free of fear. It takes a brave person to be willing to face these notions or concepts without fear, and I believe an even braver one to interact with them directly.

I will say one thing, however, and that is that some spirits who we would call "bad" will in fact present themselves as something frightening in order to scare people. It's like putting on a Halloween costume for the sheer purpose of scaring and intimidating someone. I think more than anything this is often the case with so-called demon sightings. After all, it works! People have been taught through religious means that we are to fear evil, but fear itself gives that which is evil or bad exactly what it wants and needs. What fun is it to put on a scary mask and scare someone who can't be budged? It takes the joy right out of it!

And let's take this a step further. Not only should we *not* react to the spirit attempting to trick us, but we should also offer instead a sense of compassion, love, and understanding. It's the wisdom of love which conquers all.

What do I mean by this?

If we think of this trickster spirit as someone seeking to gain control and create a reaction, then perhaps we can begin to see them merely as a wounded and powerless person. We can develop some empathy, because for whatever reason, they are so unhappy and angry that they need to take their emotions out on others — just like some people here on earth.

This doesn't mean that what they're doing is acceptable or should be tolerated, but it does mean that we can and should see them as wounded people. This requires a level of compassion on our part, asking us to see beyond the poor behavior to the pained soul behind the actions. From this vantage point we can send love to the person desiring to do us harm, and can perhaps even extend a helpful hand to the wounded soul.

No longer the enemy or the victim, we stand in a place of power that creates the potential for both ourselves and the troubled spirit to rise above the situation.

The above scenario was the opportunity made available to the negative spirit person who was harassing me. He had the chance to change his views and was offered a spiritually loving opportunity to become something more. He refused however, and was finally removed from me, never to return again. That he did not choose a better outcome for himself was his choice, but the opportunity to change was still given. This could have only come from a place of love, never from a place of defensiveness or fear.

So in the end, I personally tend to believe that it's all a game of deception and reaction. It's a case of a spirit who works to create fear and gain control at any cost, even through deception; when the reaction they desire is gained, then they hold all the power.

Can you see how this game works?

Granted it's not a game, however the process is game-like in that the spirit is seeking to take control and create an outcome of their choosing. I've been down that road, understand how this can work, but choose to reject fear and embrace compassion to create an outcome of a different nature.

If you would like to pursue this area of spiritual work, then make sure you're strong enough, smart enough, and also loving enough to do so. It is my opinion that the highest power we can have over these aggravated souls is to be compassionate and loving. If nothing else, they tend to back off in the face of these emotions which are so foreign to them, or, in a moment of grace, perhaps they'll take the chance to move on to a higher state of mind.

Summary: With all of these complaints about potential negative activity, we can see that regardless of the source, there can be a great deal of turmoil and anguish involved. If we remember to follow the 5 Major Steps for identification and resolution, then we'll be on our way to examining these matters with a little less fear. Again, the 5 Major Steps are: Acknowledge What's Happening, Remain Objective, Study and Learn, Seek Help When Needed, and Remember It's A Journey.

If by reviewing these five common complaints in addition to the 5 Major Steps, we discover a simple and reasonable explanation for our claims of negative activity, we will have gone a long way towards finding a resolution. If, however, we find that the activity is truly a negative spirit (or spirits), then the biggest question becomes one of resolution. What can we do about it?

Most of the answers can be found by examining the reason the activity began in the first place. In the next chapter, we'll look at some potential reasons these negative experiences may be occurring.

CHAPTER 6
WHY IS THIS HAPPENING?

As we look at some common reasons for why spirit activity may be occurring, I'm going to exclude the physiological or psychological reasons because I believe I've already made more than enough emphasis on how important this step is. If we now wish to consider the activity as truly a result of spirit(s) then let's look at some reasons why they may be in our life, whether the activity is negative or positive.

Reason #1: Living People – Living people are one of the main reasons for the onset of activity and can be divided into two categories: you and others. Let's look at others first.

Sometimes people note the abrupt appearance of activity when someone new moves in around them. This may especially be noted in apartment buildings and condos, but it can also involve neighborhoods. Take note of any new people near your home and watch for unusual traffic or people in your area.

Activity may also be a result of someone in your home. Ask yourself if one of the occupants has had a recent change, such as illness, tragedy, addictions, or depression. The new activity may be associated with someone in the home, even if that person has lived there for years.

Another major reason the activity may be occurring is because of children. Young children haven't been taught that spirit connection is wrong so they may be more open, welcoming, and perceptive to these events. That's not to say all children will be aware of spirits but this is always a potential to consider. Many cases of new spirit activity have been associated with children who were sensitive (intuitive, psychic, medium, etc.).

If the activity involves others, you may simply be noticing it and assuming it's for you, however, you may be its main focus. This will all depend on how the activity is occurring, so pay close attention to whom the activity is affecting and how it is affecting them. Granted, if you're the one having your hair pulled then it's probably affecting you. The question still remains whether your hair was pulled to be mean or merely to get your attention, and because you are the focus of the activity or just because you happened to be in the vicinity.

Most of us would like answers for these "whys," but the truth is we may never know. If the activity is negative, then engaging with it probably isn't something you want to do. If you are not comfortable engaging with any spirits — good or bad — that is also your choice. If you choose to embrace the activity, then we'll talk about how to potentially gain some of these answers in Chapter 8. If you prefer not to engage, we'll discuss the removal of spirit activity in Chapter 7.

Reason #2: Emerging Psychic Awareness Another reason you may be having activity is because of your awareness. I addressed this in Chapter 3. Some people are born with the ability to sense spirits. They may stifle their ability only to experience activity when it reemerges later in life. The ability is also hereditary; many adults find themselves once again having to come to terms with their awareness when they discover their children have it. If children aren't involved, then the awareness may simply be reemerging.

People who did not sense spirits as a child can also have a spontaneous emergence of awareness. This spontaneous emergence is typically a result of a wide variety of other causes which we won't get into here. Sometimes it just happens, either by conscious choice or because it was thrust upon them by circumstance.

Either way, this is probably one of the biggest reasons I see for why people are having activity. The fact that we can notice spirits may be a little jarring, but this doesn't mean the spirits are bad or intend us harm.

In addition, people with emerging awareness are generally able to notice more than one spirit and can usually discern their intentions. If you're noticing only one spirit and the activity is constant, there may be other factors involved other than awareness.

Reason #3: Location – A specific place may be the cause of the activity. This can include a piece of land, a building, or a particular location where some highly energetic event took place. The proverbial "haunted locations" that we see on TV include prisons, hospitals, battlefields, forts, old buildings, and so on.

There's something to be said for the high energetic component these sites hold, although I must say that to believe spirits are "trapped" there or are "haunting" the place may be a bit misguided.

I don't know, but if it was me and I'd passed on, a prison or hospital would be the last place I'd want to hang out. I suppose this lends validity to the fact that those who are there are somehow trapped or forced to be there.

Is it possible someone could still be looming around? Perhaps, but we need to consider the echo/imprint potential before assuming an actual presence is the cause.

If you've moved to a new location, then truth be told, you may not know the history of the place or even of nearby locations that may be affecting things. It's funny that even on real estate contracts there's a question which asks the sellers to mention any "unusual" events that may be occurring with the property, including strange activity, deaths on the site, etc. Buyers are supposed to be informed prior to a purchase if anything unusual is happening. Not everyone would actually confess to having experienced unusual activity, but you can certainly contact the previous owners and ask them about it. If you're renting then you can ask your neighbors or try asking the landlord to see if anyone made any complaints. Granted it can be a touchy subject, but if you truly want to know why and to find resolution, then you should consider this option.

The other thing you can do is check with your local Historical Society. They will know the history of many prominent locations and some will even have local legends and ghost stories they might be able to share. Of course, the library and old newspapers can also provide insights regarding events that may have transpired. You'll just have to do some research to get those answers.

Reason #4: Intention & Desire – Some people desire to see spirits and invite spirit interaction. How and why they do so critically impacts the type of experience they have. There's some wisdom to the idea that if you don't know what you're doing regarding the spirit world, then it's better to leave it alone. Opening the door to the spirit world can be like playing with fire, **BUT**, and I mean this wholeheartedly, there are also wonderful and positive interactions to be had. If you want to embrace this world, then don't sit down one night and dabble for the fun of it. Study, educate yourself, learn from others who've been there, and always stay focused on the loving and spiritual aspect.

If you do decide to open the door and invite spirit activity in, then ensure that you limit the type of people who can visit you. You wouldn't throw a party and announce it to anyone and everyone. You'd probably invite family, friends, and loved ones. Make sure you do this with spirits as well.

Here again I have to talk about the dreaded fear! If you do open the door and yet walk around in constant fear, then your very attitude is welcoming and inviting bad things to happen. Life is also like this. If you see and expect the bad, then somehow it's what you will get. Don't see or expect or fear negativity. Focus your energy on the positive and good and live that way, in life and when dealing with spirits.

Reason #5: Spirit Free Will – Upon death we do not lose our free will. We're just as capable of making a choice on the other side as we are here, which means, if someone wants to contact you then they can. Granted we can take certain precautions to protect ourselves. We work to protect our privacy in the real world, or at least we should, and likewise we should protect our privacy in our dealings with the spirit world. I'll discuss some steps for this in Chapter 8. However, no measures are fool-proof, and sometimes stuff happens that is outside of our control, just as it does in the real world!

By and large, most spirit contact is loving, peaceful, and designed to help. Family, loved ones, and other forms of guardians and protectors watch over us and may attempt to connect with us in direct ways. We should not be afraid of this contact, although we certainly have the choice of whether or not to embrace it.

And at a deeper level, if we can accept the spirit world as a real potential, then we need to recognize that some spirits are in need of our help. Just as we may turn to our loved ones in the spirit world for help, so too do some of them turn to us. This may seem odd because we've been taught that upon death suddenly life is perfect, but this isn't the case. We take our baggage with us when we go. We may have greater clarity, but we also retain our personality and often carry many of the same woes as when we were alive. Sometimes spirits want our help and will seek out those they believe can offer assistance. In this case, the activity ceases to be about us and more about the spirit.

We move from a place of victim to one of aide.

Reason #6: Higher Learning – This reason may be a tough one for some people to embrace. We often see negative events, tragedies, and bad experiences as things that shouldn't happen. While these experiences aren't pleasant, they do teach us things that positive experiences simply can't. We'd love for all our learning and growth to come from knowledge and pleasant interactions, but often courage and power come from overcoming fear and powerlessness.

The challenges we face in life, whether spirit related, physiologically or psychologically-related or otherwise, all give us the chance to rise above the moment and grow into something we weren't before the experience happened. If we can take this vantage point, even in the midst of difficult times, then we stand the chance to find the solutions we need as well as the gifts our challenges offer us. Sometimes spirit activity, good or bad, can teach us valuable life lessons, not just spiritual ones!

Reason #7: Negative Habits – This is another reason that people may not choose to accept or believe, but our negative habits in life may invite negative spirit activity. Just because we have a bad habit doesn't mean we're destined to be plagued with a spirit. That's just not true. However, some habits spiritually weaken us and open us to the *possibility* of negative activity. Let's look at an example.

As a shortcut, you always walk home from work down a dark alley at 8:00pm in a part of town where crime is high. You've done it for months and nothing has ever happened, until one night when someone mugs you, takes your money, and leaves you badly beaten. Did you deserve it? Of course not! Did you put yourself in a precarious position? Yes! Did you get mugged every night? No, but by engaging in this activity you were risking it all the same. You could have walked down this alley for years and have had nothing happen, but it is also possible that you could have been mugged on day one.

In the same way, our negative habits are not the actual cause of negative spirit activity nor do we deserve them, but it can allow things to happen. If you're looking for a reason why you have experienced negative activity, ask yourself if you're living some aspect of your life in a spiritually precarious way. Addictions of all kinds are a key example, whether they are sexually or chemically based. Other negative habits may include risk-taking behaviors, yelling or poor anger management, focusing on the negative, etc. These too can weaken us.

We should not fear things will happen because of these issues. We all face difficult times in life and many of us never have a spirit interaction. However, if you are having negative activity, then this is an area you may want to consider as a potential contributing factor and potential reason why the activity may be ongoing.

Reason #8: Spiritual Awareness – The last potential reason for spirit activity, even if it is negative activity, may be to create spiritual awareness in your life. There are many positive avenues for gaining spiritual awareness, but for some of us our awareness may be developed in other ways. It may seem cruel that God or whatever higher Power we may believe in would want us to become spiritually aware in such a difficult way; however, things happen all the time that are less than positive and which we don't always understand.

I see many people change their lives when spirit activity occurs, be it positive or negative. We're forced to consider the notion of life after death, we ponder our own existence and what that means, and we turn to a place of love and wisdom for spiritual assistance. In the end, this may in fact be the whole point!

Summary: When true spirit activity is identified, I believe it's important to ask *why*. This helps us to start working towards an understanding of what's happening, but I also want to encourage people to take that why one step further and think about *how* this pertains to your spiritual self.

Asking why you encountered spirit activity is kind of like asking *Why did I get cancer?* or *Why did I get hit by that car?* or *Why did I have to be the one to get fired?* Sometimes stuff happens and asking why allows us to make sense of things. If we can understand the "why" we can better work with it, but we shouldn't ask why from the place of being a victim. Why *not* you?

There's something deeper in the why of unusual and difficult events: there's the opportunity to grow, learn and expand, to become more than we are now and to triumph in body, mind, and spirit. Granted, we may not like the challenge, but the opportunity to grow is there if we choose to look at it this way and work to overcome the obstacles.

Heroes become heroes because of their ability to triumph over hardships and adversity, not because everything was easy.

As I've said before, if spirit activity is truly valid and it's happening to you, then ask "Why *not* you?" Don't you, like all other people, need to be shown the depth of the spirit world and what this means for your life? There is something to be learned from all experiences, whether they are positive or negative or both.

Let's also not forget that spirit activity is about another person — the spirit. We tend to forget sometimes that these events aren't just about us. This is another soul who has something to say or do, some goal or purpose in mind, and just as with people here on earth, we don't always know or understand what that is. Why it's happening may have as much to do with them as it does you, so also consider this thought when asking why.

In closing this chapter about why spirit activity may be occurring, you may wonder why I haven't offered any solutions. In truth, if we examine the reasons for the activity then we find the very answers we need to resolve it.

Maybe we can't control the location or other people but we can develop methods and set up boundaries to help us protect our spiritual privacy. We can do research and learn possible reasons why the activity is occurring. We can ensure that if we want to welcome and invite spirit activity into our life that we do so with serious intent and dedication to a loving and spiritual path. We can examine our habits, health, and lifestyle to see what changes we may need to make in order to heal and live a more positive life. We can educate ourselves, expand our horizons, and consider the notion of spirit interaction in all its forms, not just those that are negative. We can become aware of the spirit world and learn more about what it is and why it's connecting with us.

By understanding these potential reasons for activity we can start to learn how to cope with them and find resolution.

CHAPTER 7
TIPS FOR REMOVING SPIRIT ACTIVITY

Some people opt not to have spirit activity or interaction in their lives, even if it's positive. Many adults who were once sensitive to spirits when young were taught not to speak of it. I can't tell you how many people I've met who said they were aware of spirits from an early age but who were taught to ignore spirits and to not speak of their existence. Funny, the nature of life after death is one of humankind's quintessential questions, and we sweep any answers under the rug out of fear.

There's no doubt that growing up psychic/sensitive/intuitive (or whatever word you'd like to use) is a tough road. Parents want their children to be happy and normal and not to feel different or judged. Parents know how hard life can be and anything that can jeopardize that sense of normalcy is something they'd like to help their children avoid. The funny thing is, many adults who have repressed their abilities find that their children are born with the same awareness and so are again forced to contend with the issue.

I do believe that many of these parents now realize how ignoring their abilities actually created its own unique set of issues and are now working to help their children more readily embrace and deal with these events.

But perhaps we weren't aware of spirits at all, then something happened and awareness permeated our life. Or, maybe the activity is bleeding through because of someone or something else, and we simply need some steps to make it stop.

No matter the cause, we're all free to choose if we want spirit activity in our lives. Like anything else in life we choose to undertake, it has its own set of challenges as well as gifts. We don't have to embrace or accept it if we don't want to, and this is the first thing we need to understand if we want the activity to stop.

Tip #1: You Have a Choice – As I've said, we're not victims. While you may not have all the information needed to resolve the matter right away, the most powerful force you have available to you is that of **choice**. You can choose to accept or refuse the activity but you need to fully embrace a decision one way or the other and then move forward from there.

As this chapter is about removing activity, we'll assume you've decided it's not for you. The first thing you want to do is make this fact known in every way. You can do this verbally, either out loud or silently. You don't have to shout or yell or even get angry. Just be firm, loving, and confident. You also don't have to explain or justify it to anyone, spirit or living; simply state your intentions and indicate that your home as well as your personal being is a spirit-free zone.

I also suggest that you do this often — not obsessively, but perhaps on a daily or twice-daily basis until you feel the activity has stopped. Even then, you may still want to continue setting your intentions daily, or if you prefer, at least weekly or monthly.

Of course, the next question becomes: What if this doesn't work?

Tip #2: Ask for Spiritual Assistance – As ironic as it may seem, while you don't want spirit activity in your life, this doesn't mean you can't call on loving and positive spiritual forces to help support your decision. Spirits who love and care for you will honor your free will and choices and will respect your wishes — so call on their help and assistance.

I do want to add a few caveats here.

Let's say your father is recently departed and he wants to assure you he's alive and well because you're grieving heavily. He's been trying to affect your home in order to contact you, but you've decided you don't want the activity present. Will your father try harder before he gives up? Maybe he will and maybe he won't. That depends on your father and the relationship the two of you had. Maybe he'll honor your wishes right away and try again later or in another less invasive way, or maybe he'll push back trying all the more to get you to embrace his presence. Don't forget, he has free will too, and when two people with free will get together, things don't always go smoothly. The one with the stronger will tends to win.

If, however, the spirit person is someone with bad intentions, then you may want your spiritual "tribe" to come and help escort them on their way, so don't hesitate to ask for that assistance.

Asking for spiritual assistance is an important part of the process but in my experience it alone isn't always enough. Usually there are other actions that will also be required. Remember, asking for help is fine but we must also be working to do our part in the process, not just expecting or hoping others will make it go away for us.

Of course, the next question becomes: What if this doesn't work?

Tip #3: Create a Spiritually Secure Home – There are many ways you can create a home that's spiritually secure. Just as you would add a firewall and other security components to your computer, you want to safeguard your home as well. The methods you use can vary and should be ones that work for you and make you feel comfortable. For example, if you're religious, then you may want to ask a religious leader to come and bless your home or ask for a prayer group to send love and healing to your home.

If you would prefer, you could invite a Native American or Shamanic practitioner to perform a spiritual ceremony. This may involve prayers, asking for spiritual assistance on your behalf, and/or the burning of sage or other spirit offerings.

You can also perform your own ceremonies and blessings that feel right for you. Read from a religious or sacred text, light candles, and/or perform some specific action that helps you place a spiritual force-field around your home.

Maintaining the right home environment is also very important. All homes have an energetic imprint as a result of those living inside it. You can improve this energetic imprint by keeping violence and negative experiences out of your home. Negative content in TV, video games, and other seemingly passive sources can have an impact. Add love and laughter to your space. Play games, color, watch comedies, play uplifting music, unify your family, go for walks together, and have fun! Believe it or not, these simple things strengthen the spiritual security of your home.

Of course, all families and people go through tough times. If this is the case for you, take a look at how these events may be negatively impacting your space. While we may not be able to remove the tough times, we can certainly find ways to bring joy, love, hope, and strength to those moments.

While negativity can make you more susceptible to negative spirit activity, positivity helps change the energetic feel of the home, supporting a loving environment and preventing the "virus" of bad activity from getting in!

Of course, the next question becomes: What if this doesn't work?

Tip #4: Create a Spiritually Strong Self – I'm not saying you need to be religious: I am saying to be as spiritually healthy as you can. Make good choices for yourself, be kind, stay positive, remain hopeful, and find ways to overcome your limitations and challenges. Find courage you didn't know you had and work through those matters that are challenging you. Maybe this means getting help with a physiological or psychological issue, healing yourself emotionally and/or mentally, or working towards creating a sense of self that's happy and purposeful rather than sad and lost. And most of all, work to overcome any sense of fear or powerlessness you may have.

I believe all people want to be happy. I think sometimes we just don't know how to find it and/or we're not willing to work to get it. We think we'll find the right job or person to make us happy, but how long does that happiness last? Maybe shopping or having new experiences are temporarily thrilling but how long does the feeling last before we need something new to fill us up again? True joy and happiness is an inner search. The strengthening of our personal being is of value to all people, whether we find that in religion or elsewhere. By working towards and finding true joy, we can create a spiritual self that is unshakable.

Of course, the next question becomes: What if this doesn't work?

Tip #5: Ignore All Activity – At this point, if for some reason the activity still remains, then be sure you're not acknowledging it any way. If you're tracking it, why are you doing so? If you are tracking the activity because you plan to ask for assistance, make your notes brief and don't dwell on it. If you don't need to track the activity for assistance or to appease your curiosity, stop noting it. Yes, I know this is easier said than done, but if you are truly applying the above steps, then by now whatever it is should be less active or have stopped. If not, then ensure you don't acknowledge it in any way.

If some spirit is hoping to outlast you in a contest of wills and cause an issue, then even saying "Oh, there it goes again" is a form of acknowledgment. Just imagine that little kid tugging at your pant leg and begging for a piece of candy. It can be darn hard to ignore, but you have to in order to make it go away.

And don't laugh at it. This too is an acknowledgment. To truly ignore it, focus your attention on something else. Walk away, watch TV, go for a walk, play music, read a book — anything that switches your mind and attention away from whatever activity may be going on.

Of course, the next question becomes: What if this doesn't work?

Tip #6: Ask for Human Assistance – I believe in asking for help and I think there are two kinds of people when it comes to asking: those who need help for everything and those who never ask. Obviously the best course of action is somewhere in the middle.

As I've already discussed, we need to be personally proactive when working to resolve spirit activity. I highly suggest you begin with the first five tips provided in this chapter and then work yourself up to this one.

What do I actually mean by human assistance?

Asking for resources and education is not the kind of assistance I'm referring to here. I highly encourage this kind of information seeking at a very early stage. However, when you desire to stop spirit activity and the previous tips have not produced results, you may want to seek help from another person. But who?

As I mention in the section on finding a Spiritual Advocate, it is difficult to find someone who is trustworthy, believes in spirit activity, and who thinks they can remove it. You can certainly look for a religious leader as I mentioned in Tip #2. However, according to the people I've had contact with, most priests will only bless a home and little more.

Will this remove the activity?

Maybe it will and maybe it won't. Maybe the person doing the blessing isn't the right person for the job. They may be going through the actions without actually believing or bringing a true spiritual intent to the deed. Or, they may have serious spiritual intent, but it may take a few times for the blessings to work.

I also mention Shamanism as a source of assistance because this is a spiritual path that acknowledges spirits on a broader spectrum, not as simply good and evil. While for some people Shamanism may seem less than conventional, it is, however, a very ancient and well-established tradition within a variety of cultures.

Shamanism typically offers ceremonies and actions that can be performed in order to work directly with spirits and these will vary depending on the type of Shaman.

Of course, it's far easier to find a leader from an organized religion than it is a practicing Shaman. When seeking a Shaman you'll want to look at native and indigenous belief systems. In the United States this may include a Native American Shaman.

Doing some keyword searches will help you begin to find resources for these individuals. I would also highly suggest that before you hire a Shaman you ask for references, review their website, and ask pointed questions about how they can potentially assist you.

In addition to religious leaders, there are also many Psychics and Mediums who will do what is called "clearing" your home. Here too we need to be careful. It's easy to come in and say a few words and then wander out. Most people who perform blessings and clearings, including religious leaders, ask for some form of payment for the service. You should ask about prices, success rates, referrals, and how the person works as well as what they'll do if the activity continues or starts up again.

So, whether you choose a religious leader or some type of alternative Advocate, remember not all people are equal in ability and sincerity. Word of mouth is always best for finding reputable assistance, but it can still be tough. True cases of negative activity are quite rare, so those who work with these matters are as well. Do your best to resolve the activity following the previous tips, but don't be afraid to ask for help when and if you feel the time has come.

Of course, the next question becomes: What if this doesn't work?

Tip #7: Accept the Journey – This tip is not about defeat. It's about understanding that whatever is happening may take some time to be resolved. If, after following every tip, the activity persists and is truly spirit-based and not medically related, then there is more to be learned, understood, and applied.

I cannot and truly do not believe that we live in a world where spiritual assistance is not available to us. That said, we all walk through difficult times in our lives when we'd like things to be different. The solution may take time to come to fruition and you'll need to ensure that you're working towards it rather than running from it, feeling defeated, or expecting someone else to fix it for you, including someone in the spiritual world!

Summary: These suggestions may not seem like enough, but if a real spirit is causing the activity, then most often one or more of these will resolve the situation. Ideally, I recommend you apply all of them!

Now, if the matter is location-based and/or an echo, you're probably not going to have control over it or success with the tips in this chapter. In this case, relocation is the remaining option. However, relocation tends not to be a possibility, forcing people to embrace and accept the activity even if they'd prefer not to.

I also want people to know that my suggestions are based on personal experience. I've had my own interaction with a negative spirit, although I prefer to refer to it as a spiritual lesson because that's what it ended up being.

My situation lasted roughly three months. As a Medium, my experience was awareness-based involving mental harassment. As time went by, the presence seemed to have minor effects in my home but it was hard to tell if these were a result of the spirit or my own emotional turmoil. I tried many of the suggestions I've offered here, and in the end, over time, a combination of all of these things finally worked.

I share this story because I want people to realize that not only am I giving these suggestions as someone who believes and works with spirit, but also as someone who has experienced negative activity. I often see people who do either paranormal work or Mediumship-type work, who offer advice on negative experiences without any background or personal experience. Their information may be quite valid, but sometimes it's based on a belief and not experience. Once again, someone's spiritual resume and experience should speak to their level of knowledge on these matters, so ask about their background and where their knowledge comes from before trusting fully.

I also want to add that I truly believe that one of the two major reasons why my experience occurred was so that I could be an Advocate for others. As someone who walks and works in the spiritual world, how could I possibly assist others without some level of first-hand knowledge? Knowing a thing and experiencing it are vastly different. Without the actual interaction, I could not fully understand the emotional and mental strain which accompanies these events, or even the post-traumatic stress which follows once it's finally gone.

The second reason my situation occurred was because I asked for it — but let me clarify this! I didn't say, "Hey, I want some bad spirit to show up and harass me." What I did ask was to be able to better understand the mindset of negative spirits and to understand what we refer to as "bad" or "evil." Of course, I'd hoped for a more intellectual understanding, but I couldn't have truly understood this concept without the actual experience. Looking back, I'm grateful for it as it has made me spiritually stronger and has allowed me to more deeply understand these events when they occur to others.

My way is certainly not the only way of dealing with unwanted activity, positive or negative. There are many wonderful Spiritual Advocates out there, so please seek education and wisdom from a wide variety of sources, not just my own. Others may also offer some excellent views and considerations that I haven't covered here.

Education is empowerment!

CHAPTER 8
TIPS FOR EMBRACING SPIRIT ACTIVITY

Surprisingly, many people welcome spirit activity and interaction. They may not talk about or admit this freely, but for them it's positive, uplifting, and even comforting. This is true whether the activity is a result of simple awareness or observation. We each see spirit activity differently and have unique experiences with it.

If you're one of those people who would like to embrace the activity — or find yourself unable to relocate from it — then here are some tips you can implement to help you coexist in peace with these events.

Tip #1: Set Boundaries - For those who are excited to explore spirit activity, don't pursue it so enthusiastically that you start to become unbalanced. It's important to set boundaries for yourself as well as for the spirits. As excited as you may be about the potential interactions, don't let them consume you or your personal life.

If you want to learn and explore, then set aside strict times to do so. You should make these times known and expect spirits to respect them as well. If you're being woken up, then ask them to stop and to connect with you at a time that doesn't disrupt your sleep. If you feel spirits are trying to connect with you during your personal time, then politely explain that you're not to be disturbed right now.

What this does mean, however, is that you do need to make time to allow those interactions to occur. If you maintain a dedicated time for connection, then you'll typically find that the activity will only occur when you're ready. However, if you ignore the contact, then the spirits may push your boundaries in order to remind you of their presence and the promised interaction time.

How you set boundaries and make time for appropriate interactions will also vary depending on how you're noticing the activity. If you have emerging awareness, then you may need to meditate, journal, sketch, doodle, or perform some other task that helps you get into a state of awareness that allows for connection. Even if you are able to connect without this intermediary step, you should designate specific times for spirit interaction. This gives your mind and body a break and doesn't "invite" the interaction to occur at any time of the day or night.

If, on the other hand, you're observing the activity and it's occurring in your environment, you will still want to set up some rules. Ask the spirits to be quiet when you're sleeping, to find ways to connect without frightening or alarming the children, and to not create an issue when company arrives. These are just examples, of course, so set those boundaries that work for you in your home.

Some people ask if they can record audio or video in their home. I think this is an excellent question but one which each person will need to decide for themselves. A word of caution: just remember that by opening the door to this type of interaction, you're potentially inviting more activity. Don't do this without setting clear boundaries and guidelines for who can connect with you, and when and why they can. You should only seek to connect with positive people for your learning and education.

I would also recommend you perform a ceremony or offer some prayers to create a space that allows the right environment for these types of interactions. As silly as it may seem, it's the dabbling and lack of knowledge, however innocent, which can get people into trouble.

And finally, you also need to set boundaries for yourself. Always remember to maintain balance. As wonderful as the spirit connection process may be, opening up too fast and too wide can cause problems in your physical life. Both the spiritual and physical are important, so be sure to honor each accordingly.

Tip #2: Study, Study, Study – Experience is an amazing teacher, but it's not enough. If you opt to welcome activity, then do so responsibly and learn more about it. Read and study the experiences of others, and work to understand spirits and spirit communication. Sometimes we leap to conclusions about our experiences and assume them to be true for all interactions, forgetting that spirits are people too and each interaction will be unique.

I especially emphasize this tip if you're someone who's aware (in other words a psychic, intuitive, or medium-depending on what word feels best for you). Take classes, read, join groups, and look for forums or other ways to interact with those having the same experiences. This can help you not only learn, but also to not feel so alone or fearful. "Coming out" in regards to one's psychic abilities is often very tough, but it's a necessary step on the road to education.

Tip #3: Positive Spirit Activity Only – Just as you should surround yourself with the right people here in this world, you need to do the same with the spirit world. Setting an intention to only have loving and positive spirit interactions is important. I personally like to invite my loved ones in spirit and those that are only for my "highest good" to come hang out, should they feel the need. I invite interaction at certain times of the day and night and expect to be left alone at others. In addition, I ask my loved ones in spirit to help safeguard my home and person from those who don't meet my welcome "criteria."

Some people also like to ask other higher forms of spirits to visit or help safeguard their home and person. This will be different for everyone and can range from guides, angels, saints, to God or other religious figures. It really depends on your belief system and what makes you feel comfortable. Just remember to ask!

Tip #4: Spirit Protection – I'm often asked about protection, and while I do believe this is important, I also don't think you should obsess about it. It seems that those who obsess and are adamant about strict protection rituals also tend to be the ones who harbor the most fear. In other words, their concern is so great that the ritual is actually performed out of fear rather than out of a place of love and simply asking for spiritual protection.

I believe I've addressed precautionary measures you can take all throughout the book, including: setting intentions for only positive spirits, creating a loving home and environment, and also creating a loving and spiritual self — mentally, emotionally, and physically.

When it comes to ceremony or rituals, these too will depend on the person. I enjoy lighting candles and saying prayers. Every culture and belief system has a wide range of practices which can be used for setting up a protecting and loving space, so use those that feel right for you.

Tip #5: Validation – When embracing spirit activity based on awareness, validation is another critical step. Many people feel they are hearing or seeing spirits and find this confusing as well as frightening. If you've chosen to embrace the activity, then in order to better understand it you need to start utilizing your awareness with and for others.

Validation is the crucial process of realizing your awareness is based in reality, not imagination. The more validation you gain from others regarding your awareness and abilities, the greater comfort you take in spirit activity. This allows you to better embrace the activity and to grow alongside it with greater confidence and certainty.

Tip #6: The Spiritual Path – The last thing I want to add regarding embracing spirit activity is to remember that it's not a curiosity or a freak show, nor is it a path to fame, fortune, or notoriety. If spirit activity is real, then you need to consider what this implication truly means, for those in spirit as well as for yourself.

Your connections with spirit activity are about the spiritual path, the awareness that you are more than your physical body and that life is beyond the now. They also show you that love never dies and the connections you have with those who matter are eternal. You need to remember that these interactions are here to teach you something deeper about your existence. This is the truth that should reside at the core of your heart and mind during your interactions with spirit.

Summary – When it comes to embracing spirit activity, some people may be undecided. One aspect which can inform their choice may be to determine who is causing the activity. Beyond the "why" of spirit activity , the next biggest question people want to know is "who". After all, if we knew who it was, perhaps we could rest easier or converse with them with greater awareness.

When trying to find out who a spirit is, the best course of action you can take is to ask the spirit directly, then wait and watch for clues. People tend to rush to find a Medium, and this is fine, but who's to say who or what the Medium will sense once they arrive? Maybe the Medium will be able to detect who the spirit person is around you, but then again, maybe they won't. Maybe the spirit won't talk to the Medium because their identity is for you to discover or because they want to keep who they are hidden. (The latter is more common in land or location based scenarios.)

If the activity is not an echo and is truly caused by a spirit, then all you can do is ask. You can't force them, however, no more than you can force a stranger to tell you their name. The best you can do is create an honest, caring, and respectful relationship with the spirit and/or start the process of getting them to leave.

If the activity is caused by a loved one, then you'll probably find at some level that you'll be able to figure this out. I recall one home where the occupants always heard the cabinet doors and pots and pans banging, but no matter what they did they couldn't actually observe this happening, they could only hear it. They called me in, and I began to describe the person I felt was responsible — who they quickly identified with a resounding "Aha." It was a recently deceased father who loved to cook and always spent his time in the kitchen. This was his way of letting them know he was still around and still "cooking" even though he wasn't there in human form.

Had they thought about it, they probably could have come to this conclusion on their own. Granted, it's nice to have the validation, but we need to understand that just because we call in a Medium or Psychic doesn't mean they can always confirm who someone is or even why they're there.

Embracing spirit activity is as simple as deciding you want it to be a part of your life. However, the effects of that decision can be far-reaching. Some people choose to embrace spirit activity because of the comfort it provides them, others for curiosity, and some because it becomes a way of life to provide spirit messages and awareness to those around them. No matter the reasoning behind the embrace, it becomes a life-long process of learning, exploring, and understanding. Education and experience, as well as openness, allows us to learn and better understand the world of spirits.

Conclusion
What Is Spirit Activity?

By now, you may be wondering if I've actually answered the titular question, "What Is Spirit Activity?"

The truth is that there is not one answer: real spirit activity can take many forms and can be noticed in a wide variety of ways. Then there are those unexplained events which are claimed to be spirit-related, but which most likely result from physical causes. Determining their true origin becomes a matter of interpretation and may require additional knowledge. Even experts may not ultimately agree about the cause of the activity.

We're blessed to live in a country where freedom of belief and expression is a right. As someone who has served to defend that freedom, I want to stress that I believe my views expressed in this guide are just that — my views. However, these views are informed by my genuine and extensive experience. Our judgment of experience may be fallible, but by what other means can we begin to understand and explain a phenomenon that can't be seen?

The truth of spirit activity is found by examining our experiences objectively. At some point we should be capable of defending our experience with some form of rationale and proof, not just belief. Of course, hard proof can be difficult to come by in a field that demands some measure of belief, but a well-executed examinational process in conjunction with rational and objective considerations will go much further when arguing a case than a "because I believe it to be true" statement.

So, while many of us will claim spirit activity and believe in it to the bitter end, others will deny it with the same vehemence. Ideally, we should fall somewhere in the middle and allow continued exploration to be our goal, not simply the defense and vindication of our personal views. Through exploration and understanding we find the answers regarding these events. In other words, we find the truth by admitting what we **don't** know, not what we do.

I hope that what I've shared in this Resource Guide will provide a process for evaluating unexplained activity, as well offering possible solutions and avenues for exploration. I've seen too many people seeking answers for these events and not knowing where to turn or what to do.

Whether a claim is well-founded or based in environmental phenomena or physiological or psychological issues, people are in need of information and assistance. As a Spiritual Advocate, I offer this book to all those seeking answers. May it be helpful on their path — and yours!

APPENDIX - INTERVIEW QUESTIONS & RESOURCES

Paranormal Questionnaire

Here is a list of suggested questions you may want to ask a potential paranormal group before you allow them to help you with your situation. Allow their answers to help guide you towards choosing the group that best fits for you.

1. Do you believe in spirits?
   a. If so, how do you validate spirit activity?
   b. If not, then what evidence would you need to consider the activity to be valid?
2. What is your group's overall theory and ideology regarding spirit activity? (Including: ghosts, trapped souls, hauntings, evil spirits, friendly spirits, and life after death)
3. What can I expect from an investigation?
4. How many people will come to my home/location?
5. What equipment do you use and why?
6. Will I receive follow-up contact and if so how?
7. Will I receive the results of your investigation in writing?
   a. If so, do you have an example of what I can expect?

b. If not, then does this mean you did not find any evidence?

8. Will you remove the activity for me?
9. Will you communicate with the activity?
10. Can you tell me who is causing the activity?
11. Will you confirm if my home/location is haunted?
12. Do you have liability insurance?
13. Do you do research on my location, and if so, how?
14. Will I receive information regarding your location research findings?
15. How many investigations has your group conducted?
16. How much experience does the team working on my case have? Is anyone new or in-training?
17. Can I be present for the investigation?
18. What are some of the common causes of activity that are not spirit-related?
19. Do you have any educational resources you can recommend to assist me with my situation?
20. Once the investigation is over, what kind of follow-up care do you offer, if any?
21. Do you charge for your services?

Spiritual Advocate Questionnaire

Here is a list of suggested questions you may want to ask a potential Intuitive, Medium, or Psychic before you allow them to help you with your situation. Allow their answers to help guide you towards choosing an Advocate that best fits for you.

1. Do you believe in spirit activity?
2. What is your overall theory and ideology regarding spirit activity? (Including: ghosts, trapped souls, hauntings, evil spirits, friendly spirits, and life after death)
3. What religious and/or spiritual framework best explains your personal ideology and beliefs?
4. Do you believe all spirits are bad?
5. Do you believe spirit communication and interaction is possible?
6. Do you believe in Mediums? Why or why not?
7. Will you communicate with the spirit for me?
8. If so, how, and how will I know if what you're telling me is accurate?
9. Will you remove the spirits for me?
10. Can you fix the problem for me?
11. What theories and knowledge do you have regarding activity that may not be based on spirits?

12. What educational resources and tools can you offer me regarding my situation?
13. What process will you use to assist me, and how long does this process last?
14. Do you charge for your services?
15. What guarantees do I have regarding the services you provide?
16. If you say you can remove the activity but it comes back do you repeat your service? If so, what costs are involved?
17. What type(s) of after-care and follow-up assistance do you offer?
18. What is your experience and background with spirit activity?
19. How long have you been doing this work?
20. Why do you do this work?
21. How long will all of this take?

Appendix

Steps to Help Maintain a Spiritually Secure Home

1. Have your location blessed or cleansed by someone who does this as a part of their spiritual service.
2. Bless or cleanse the home yourself.
3. Focus on only inviting spiritual assistance of the type and intent of your choosing. For example, positive, loving, family, angels, saints, God, a religious leader of your choosing, etc.
4. Ask for spiritual protection and guidance from the sources listed above.
5. Do not perform any of the above actions in fear, but rather from a place of love and with the knowledge that you are loved and supported even if it doesn't feel like it at this very moment.
6. Perform a daily spiritual ceremony that helps you to feel safe, focused, shares your intentions, and reinforces your boundaries and desires: prayer, meditation, singing, dancing, reciting from a spiritual text, lighting candles, drumming or music, etc.
7. Maintain positive activities in the home: play, laughter, fun, joy, sharing, connection with all members of the family, harmony, etc.
8. Remove activities that do not support the above: violence, distance, disconnection, anger, antagonizing, fear, judgment, etc.

Steps to Help Maintain a Spiritually Secure Self

1. Focus on only inviting spiritual assistance of the type and intent of your choosing: positive, loving, family, angels, saints, God, a religious leader of your choosing, etc.
2. Maintain a healthy body and use medications, chemicals, stimulants and other drugs only as needed and/or in moderation.
3. Maintain a well-balanced state of mind. Work to remain positive, confident, and avoid negative thoughts or intentions.
4. Maintain a well-balanced emotional self. Work to stay happy, joyful, hopeful, and positive. Invite love and be kind, avoiding anger and fear at all costs.
5. Balance your spiritual and physical self. Walk, garden, exercise, enjoy nature, take up a hobby, dance, sing, laugh, have fun. On the other hand, pray, meditate, read uplifting and inspiring materials, study, learn, and interact with others who share your spiritual ideologies. Both of these aspects of our self matter, so honor them accordingly.

Keywords to Research

Spiritual Emergence, Spiritual Crisis, Spiritual Awakening

Spiritual Psychology, Spiritual Counseling

Transpersonal Psychology

Psychologist, Therapist, Psychiatrist, Counselor

Parapsychology, Parapsychologist

Paranormal Studies

Paranormal Activity (not the movie) or Spirit Activity

Paranormal Groups or Societies

Consciousness, Mind, Brain

Brain Games, Brain Self Deception, Pareidolia

Consciousness Studies

Awareness, Spiritual Awareness

Intuitive, Medium, Psychic

Brain Wave Patterns, Brain Wave States, Altered States

Sleep Disorders, Sleep Apnea, Sleep Paralysis

Spiritual Protection, Psychic Protection

Spiritual Ceremonies and Rituals (add the religion of your choice to these words)

Home Cleansing and Blessing

New Age, Metaphysical, Shamanism

Resources & Links

Please do your own research regarding the resources below. I do not personally endorse any of them, nor am I compensated by them in any way. They're simply here to give you tools to get started looking for answers.

Spiritual Emergence Network

Psychology Today Therapists

Parapsychological Association

Paranormal Societies

The Institute of Noetic Sciences

TED (Topics of Consciousness & Spirituality)

Society for Shamanic Practitioners

Suicide Prevention Lifeline

ACKNOWLEDGMENTS

I would like to give special thanks to the Washington State Ghost Society and all of its caring and dedicated people. As a member since May of 2012, my involvement with them as an investigator as well as a Medium (or a Sensitive as we refer to them) has been invaluable. By working directly with clients and serving as the group's email monitor, I came to realize the deep need people have to understand potential spirit activity. As a Medium my views can be biased, but as an investigator my role is to be unbiased and to become that Spiritual Advocate people need during these often difficult times.

As always, I must thank my husband for encouraging my spiritual life and allowing me to explore all of the many avenues and twists and turns it's taken us on. It's not been easy on either of us, but without his support my work would not be mentally, emotionally, or physically possible. Saying thank you will never be enough. You are my soulmate, now and always, and I will love you forever.

To my amazing Editor, Elizabeth. You helped me to understand the mechanics of writing and to become a better writer. You gave of yourself freely and took a scattered manuscript and turned it into something I'm truly proud of. You are as much a part of this work as I, and I am deeply in your debt.

To those special and dearest others who have also helped me walk this path and still are: Anne M., Dave K., Debbie K., Jeffrey M., Sarah C., Terri M., and Terri S. Each and every one of you have been there in one way or another and have helped make me who I am today — and all for the better! My undying love and gratitude to you all, as well as my eternal friendship, in this life and the next!

Lastly, to those amazing people I call my spiritual "tribe": I have been blessed with so many of them on my journey, some still present and others who have moved on but are not forgotten. They're truly genuine heartfelt people working to do good things in the world, each in their own unique way. That we've touched each other's lives in one form or another is a gift I'll always be grateful for. Thank you for being you and sharing that wonderful you with me: Betty R., Dena M., Elle G., Grace K., Heidi M., Jennifer B., Judy M., Kiran A., Leah B., Leah T., Les S., Penny C., and Stacy C.

To my family, both here and beyond: I am the one who always walked her own path, her own way, and in a manner vastly unique from those around me. It has never been easy for me, nor have I been easy for others. This does not diminish my love for all of you, even though at times it has made our connections difficult. You are always in my heart and mind, the bond of family holding you dear even as my path takes me away and in a direction I can neither ignore nor deny. You are loved!

Sometimes we forget our blessings until we look around at the people who love us. That's when we realize we have everything we could possibly ever need in this life — and more!

With all my love & gratitude,

Carol

CAN I ASK A FAVOR?

If you enjoyed this book, found it useful or otherwise, then I'd really appreciate it if you would send me a short review to info@carolgeiler.com. I read all the reviews personally so that I can continually write about what people are looking for regarding their spiritual experiences, exploration, and growth.

Thank you for your support!

ABOUT THE AUTHOR

CAROL GEILER

Spiritual Advocate & Intuitive Medium

FIND OUT MORE AT WWW.CAROLGEILER.COM

WITH A B.S. FROM SOUTHERN ILLINOIS UNIVERSITY, CAROL SERVED 4 YEARS IN THE U.S. NAVY, HELD VARIOUS MANAGEMENT POSITIONS WITH MAJOR RETAIL CHAINS, AS WELL AS SERVING AS A LOAN OFFICE AND FINANCIAL COUNSELOR BEFORE COMING ACROSS HER SPIRITUAL PATH. SINCE THAT TIME SHE HAS CREATED AND CONDUCTED CLASSES, WORKSHOPS, & SUPPORT GROUPS FOCUSED ON SPIRITUAL COMMUNICATION AND SPIRITUAL LIVING. SHE IS A CO-FOUNDER AND PAST FACILITATOR OF THE NORTHWEST MEDIUMSHIP ASSOCIATION, WAS CO-PRODUCER & CO-HOST OF THE INTERNET TALK RADIO SHOW "EXPLORERS OF CONSCIOUSNESS" AND IS AN ACTIVE MEMBER OF THE WASHINGTON STATE GHOST SOCIETY.

TODAY SHE IS A SPIRITUAL ADVOCATE, SPEAKER, WRITER, & INTUITIVE MEDIUM. HER TRUE PASSION IS WORKING WITH OTHERS TO HELP THEM THROUGH THEIR OWN SPIRITUAL JOURNEY, HOWEVER THAT LOOKS FOR THEM, AND TO HELP THEM FIND THE ANSWERS AND SOLUTIONS THEY NEED TO SUCCEED IN LIFE. SHE'S ALSO COMMITTED TO BRINGING FORTH INFORMATION AND MESSAGES FROM THE SPIRITUAL WORLD IN ORDER TO HELP OTHERS LIVE BETTER LIVES HERE IN THIS ONE!

Made in the USA
San Bernardino, CA
11 April 2016